The
Rogue Husband

Diana Elizabeth Tebbutt

Typeset in Palatino

Editing, design, typesetting and publishing by UK Book Publishing

www.ukbookpublishing.com

ISBN: 978-1-915338-07-5

The Rogue Husband

Diana Elizabeth Tebbutt

I must thank *Tania* for her help and encouragement in writing this book.

The Wonderment of Love

The wonderment of love,
Is to give and to receive,
The wonderment of love,
Is to trust and to believe.

It is not a transient magic,
That floats away like dust,
It is tangible and steadfast,
Hold on to it, one must.

But love it has its downside,
Because when we truly care,
In its wake it brings heartache,
And often bleak despair.

When we give all our feeling,
Into another's hold,
To care so much may break a heart,
With misery untold.

It is said it's better to have loved,
Than never love at all,
That may be so, but teardrops,
May also readily fall.

Love encompasses many things,
The wonderment of this world,
A baby's cry, the surge of tide,
All wonders that unfold.

The love of all the creatures,
Whether they be large or small,
The wonderment of life and love,
To be beheld by all.

But as I sit and muse,
And see the heavens above,
I only hope that I can feel
The wonderment of love.

DEL 2018

Chapter 1

Anne came home from Church Choir. It had been a very busy day at school. The Headmaster had been particularly unpleasant. He had not wanted her as his Deputy, but the Vicar, Chair of Governors, had hoped she would train his choir and she had got the job. At every opportunity the Headmaster tried to put her down, but she loved her class and loved the job. As it was a Church School, part of the job was indeed to take Church Choir, where many of her pupils were now choristers. It was 8.30pm. Robert's car was not on the drive. "Surely he should be home by now," she thought. A horrible worry came over her. Lately he had been getting back from London later and later. He had been made redundant three months earlier from his job in Coventry and despite numerous applications had not managed to secure a job locally. He had eventually obtained a job in London and assured her the hour journey by train would be no problem. Anne loved her detached house in Kenilworth and despite the Headmaster's ill will, was happy in her job. She also knew that property in London was extortionate.

At first all seemed well, but Anne was bothered when on Christmas Eve, Robert still did not return from London (he was working for a computer firm) until late evening. Anne knew that on Christmas Eve, firms shut early and when Robert came in late she said, "Why are you so late? Everyone closes early on Christmas Eve."

"I was searching for a present for you," Robert replied.

Anne was sceptical, particularly as on Christmas Day, no special present emerged. Anne also noticed that Robert was becoming irritable and bad tempered. She put it down to the stress of a new job. They had met at university in Leicester, were engaged for two years, and now married for thirteen years.

Materialistically they had done well; they now had a detached house in a lovely part of Kenilworth and two cars. It had been a blow when he lost his job – redundant because the firm shut down.

As she slowly got out of the car, she still expected to hear the sound of his car, which would have to come from Coventry Station Car Park, from where he caught his train to London.

Anne put her key in the door, went through the hall and into the kitchen. She turned on the light. There on the central heating boiler was a piece of white paper and a £20 note. Puzzled, she looked at the paper. On it was written a few words.

"I have taken the irrevocable step of leaving you,"

Robert.

Stunned, Anne went upstairs and opened the wardrobe door. All Robert's clothes had gone. She went downstairs to the bureau. The savings book had also gone.

Shocked, Anne went to the phone (there was no mobile at this time) and phoned her parents in Wellingborough. She was shaking and devastated. Her parents had no car, but her father, Howard, immediately said, "Make yourself a cup of tea. I will come to you."

Anne was so dazed she just sat down and waited. Had she seen it coming? Robert had had a brief fling with an office girl ten years previously. She had come across him writing a letter.

"Dear Joan. I love you. I love you. I love you."

He had passed it off as a bit of stupidity. Throughout their engagement Robert had never strayed, but they had been studying in Leicester, and could not meet frequently. Robert had never seemed very passionate, but Anne thought as he was an academic it was just the way he was. They had played tennis, attended concerts and gone to the picture house. Anne had been to his home in Carshalton, Surrey, and never then had cause to doubt that theirs would be a marriage for life. They had married at 21 and 22.

Robert's first position, after leaving university in July, was in Coventry. Anne obtained a teaching position there so she could be with him. They were living in separate rented accommodation, and this was expensive. They decided to marry in the December and live together in one rented flat. Anne's parents, Howard and Elizabeth, were very dubious about this young marriage, but as Anne was their only child they organised a big wedding in Wellingborough with a reception at the Hind Hotel. At this time Anne and Robert had no savings and Anne bought an 'off the peg' wedding dress of cream brocade. Robert sported a new grey suit. But of course, as time progressed with two salaries, they were able to get a mortgage and of course buy the lovely detached house in Kenilworth. Anne's mother initially lent them the money for a car as Robert had passed his driving test at 17. Robert had taught Anne to drive and now they had two cars, a Ford Zephyr and a lovely red Spitfire. Life was good, Anne thought.

CHAPTER 2

Anne's father finally arrived, and Anne sobbed into his arms.

"We will go to bed," Howard said. "And in the morning, we will go to London to see Robert. We know where he works. Phone your school in the morning and explain that you cannot come in. Tell them why."

They went to bed, and Anne's father slept in the largest room (there were four bedrooms), but Anne in her room could not sleep. Stupidly she had thought that marriage was for life. They had been married in All Hallows Church, Wellingborough, and she had believed in 'For better or worse', 'Till death do us part'. Robert had always been a quiet, serious person, but she remembered his early affair and the letter, 'Love you, love you', to Joan.

In the morning they set out for London. They found a restaurant near to Robert's work at London University Computing Service. Howard sat Anne down at a table and said he would go to the firm. After a while, Howard returned with a pale faced Robert. Howard asked Robert where he was staying.

"At the Blue Orchid Hotel," he muttered.

Howard and Robert had something to eat – beans on toast and coffee – but Anne could eat nothing. After much persuading by Howard, Robert agreed to return to Kenilworth on Saturday. This day was Tuesday. He could initially give no reason for leaving, but admitted that instead of going to work on Monday, he had waited until Anne left for school and then went back to the house to collect his belongings.

His excuse later, was that he found the journey to London trying and was having a sort of breakdown. With the promise of the weekend visit, Anne and her father left for Coventry and then to Kenilworth. Howard had to return to his wife, Elizabeth, who was equally shocked and upset at events. Anne told her mother on the phone that Robert had the savings books and Elizabeth, canny with money, told her to contact the bank and freeze that joint account.

"All you think about is money," said Anne.

"You have to be practical," said Elizabeth.

"He's coming back on Saturday," stated Anne. "Everything may still work out. Obviously, the journey has got him down. It must be very tiring driving to the station, catching a train to London, then going to the office. It is in Gordon Square, quite a way from Waterloo. He said he could easily do it, but apparently not."

"You are in denial," retorted Elizabeth. "He has taken all his personal belongings."

Anne still retorted, "He's coming back on Saturday. He promised he would come."

"Yes, but for how long? His note I believe said irrevocable and that means just that," said Elizabeth.

Anne was in denial and only thinking of seeing Robert at the weekend. She did, however, contact the bank, but that meant she only had £20 to last until the end of the month, when her salary would be paid now into her own account. Luckily, it was only a week until the end of the month. Her father had paid for the trip to London and kindly gave her another £20 before he left.

Anne's neighbour noticed Anne had not been to school and knocked to ask if everything was alright. Anne, still shocked and tearstained, told them what had happened. To her amazement, Mrs Goff did not seem sympathetic.

"What are you going to do?" she asked.

"Robert is coming back at the weekend," replied Anne.

"What made him leave like this?" enquired Mrs Goff.

It seemed as if Mrs Goff thought Anne responsible for Robert's actions.

"I am still in shock," said Anne.

"You must have had some idea, surely?" It seemed as if Mrs Goff sneered.

"He had been coming home later," replied Anne, "but he said there had been late work meetings. I noticed he was a bit irritable, but I thought it was the journey."

"Well, I am surprised," said Mrs Goff. "We always thought Robert was a lovely man. Kind and thoughtful. A perfect gentleman."

Anne didn't feel that Mrs Goff had any sympathy for her. She had taught her son Martin the piano on Saturdays in her spare time and didn't feel that this was the comfort she needed. She almost sensed a hostility, which puzzled her.

"Are you going to school tomorrow?" enquired Mrs Goff.

"I must," said Anne.

"Oh well," said Mrs Goff. "Perhaps it will all work out," and so saying she left. (She actually never spoke again to Anne. If Anne went into the garden and Mrs Goff was in her garden, she just turned away.)

It was obvious that the Goffs thought so highly of Robert, that they felt she must have done something quite disgraceful to make him leave.

Chapter 3

When Anne returned to school (an Infant and Junior school on the outskirts of Coventry), as she walked into the staffroom for an early morning coffee, the staff there seemed to be staring at her with undisguised interest. Anne said nothing. The Headmaster, Mr Roberts, came in. He seemed to glare at Anne, but he too said nothing. At the school bell Anne went into her classroom and the day progressed well. The Headmaster had taken the class during her absence and the children seemed to accept that. They perhaps thought she had been unwell. Once in the classroom, Anne was happy. They were a lovely class of mixed juniors aged 10-11.

At lunchtime Anne again sensed that the staff appeared distant, but there was a PTA meeting about possible Bingo for funds that evening, so the talk hinged on that.

Anne drove home before the meeting and it seemed strange to think that Robert was not coming home that evening. Her brain seemed numb, but she got changed and returned to the school for the meeting. It was also partly a social occasion and the school secretary had laid on coffee, tea and biscuits. There were already quite a few parents there, but as Anne walked in, they were certainly staring at her. Obviously, the reason for her absence yesterday had been leaked, and was now being gossiped about. The leak no doubt came from Mr Roberts, the Headmaster. She saw people staring at her, and her head swam and the floor seemed to tip. The Headmaster addressed the meeting. It was fairly informal with questions from the floor, but Anne felt decidedly uncomfortable. She supposed as Deputy Head she was good for local gossip, but it almost appeared as if she herself had committed some crime.

Parents were not speaking to her as before and in fact seemed to be avoiding her. Anne tried to initiate conversation with some of the mothers who had children in her class, but it was a struggle. The meeting was, as stated, mainly concerned with the holding of Bingo nights at the school to raise money for the School Fund. One parent agreed to run this on a Wednesday evening. The meeting broke up and Anne drove home.

She replayed the evening in her mind. When she had previously attended Parent Functions, everyone had wanted to speak to her. When she was appointed, she was 32. She had been the new 'image' for the school. She was tall and attractive, with fairly long golden hair. She was bubbly and dynamic and quite a few of the fathers had tried to flirt with her. She was later respected as an excellent teacher, and of course now in charge of the Church Choir. She had taken the girls to netball matches and rounders. In her first year she had taken her class to London, for a class outing, which had included a visit to Hampton Court Palace via a river trip.

Now she seemed like a pariah. She was determined, however, that this new attitude from the parents would not affect her teaching or her love for the children.

The week went on. Unfortunately, as it was January, it was very cold, and Anne was worried that if it snowed, Robert may not drive home as promised. There was a slight fall of snow, but Saturday came. Anne put on her nicest dress, thinking this could help to sway Robert to stay.

At 11am on Saturday he drove up. He obviously still had a key and walked in. He looked pale and just lay down on the settee without speaking.

"Are you really staying at 'The Blue Orchid Hotel'?" Anne asked.

"No, I am with Marilyn."

"Who is Marilyn?"

"An administrator from New Zealand now working at LUCS."

"Where does she live?"

"It doesn't matter. It's a sort of flat. A bedsit/studio type."

"Why have you left?" asked Anne.

"I have been unhappy for some time. I haven't loved you for 12 years. All you think about is school. Also, the journey to London has got me down," replied Robert.

Anne could not think of anything in reply. He was so definite. She tried to be conciliatory.

"Would you like something to eat?"

"Just a sandwich. I can't stay long. We are going out tonight."

Anne felt dead inside. Now she knew why Robert had been coming home late from London. It had obviously been planned for some time. Possibly on Christmas Eve when he came home late. Robert had never seemed too interested in sex. Once when she had suggested it, he had said, "Must you." But Anne thought because he was clever (he had gained a County Major Scholarship for Leicester), his mind was on higher things.

Anne made a ham sandwich and coffee, but Robert just stayed on the settee. He seemed to have developed a nervous tic in his cheek and certainly appeared uncomfortable. He went upstairs to the bedroom phone. Anne heard him talking.

"Oh yes, I shall be there for this evening. I am not staying long. I am only here because I promised her father."

His tone then went quiet and Anne couldn't hear the rest of the conversation.

"I'm having a bath," he called out.

Anne waited until he redressed and came down.

"Can we go out?" she asked. She thought if they went out somewhere maybe things could get back to normal.

"No! I have to get back."

Anne's heart sank into her boots. It all seemed hopeless.

"Will you come again?"

"I'll come next Saturday and stay longer."

"Must you go?" Anne pleaded.

"I need some space. I can't do that journey anymore. You have your school, and why have you frozen our account?"

"My mother suggested it."

"Well, there can't be much in the bank at present anyway. You can have it. I will organise it."

"Do you want a divorce?" asked Anne, hoping that he would immediately deny this.

"I don't know. I will come next week. Book seats at Stratford Theatre. There's bound to be a Shakespeare play there. I will come at eleven, but now I must go. Goodbye."

So saying, Robert walked rapidly to the door and left Anne in disbelief.

CHAPTER 4

O n Sunday Anne drove to her parents in Wellingborough. Her mother was still upset as she too had thought Robert a quiet and gentle person. It all seemed so out of the character in which they had come to believe.

Elizabeth had had cancer of the bowel some years previously and spent time in Northampton Hospital. Robert and Anne had visited her every evening after work. When Elizabeth recovered, Robert had driven the family to Bournemouth where they stayed several times in 4- and 5-star hotels. As Robert drove, and paid for petrol, Elizabeth had paid the hotel bills. They used to picnic on the way down to the sea and all enjoyed the break. Elizabeth was grateful for the support Robert had given, and had grown very fond of him. She too felt that the world had turned upside down. She was practical, however, and promised Anne that she need not worry about losing the house, as she would pay off the mortgage, if a divorce became inevitable.

Anne hadn't really thought that far ahead, but told her parents that Robert seemed very 'detached', and that he was involved with a girl called Marilyn with whom he was living in a studio flat.

Elizabeth, whilst offering help, also seemed to think Anne had done something wrong and she too, as others, was now cooler towards Anne. She couldn't believe that Robert would leave his lovely detached house in Kenilworth and move in with another girl in a studio flat. She felt it was totally out of character, and was concerned that he was so unhappy with Anne he had felt compelled to leave. She had thought that their marriage was perfect, and had eventually been so proud that her daughter was a teacher, and married to a clever man. She loved the house at Kenilworth and after her initial misgivings thought Robert was the perfect husband. He did not shout, and was always so polite and courteous.

"Why did this have to happen?" she asked Anne. "This hasn't happened before to anyone in our family. I thought you were nicely settled at Kenilworth. When my nephew, Buster, visited you last year from Canada, he said you had the best house in the family. Everything seemed all right then."

The church bells began to ring from All Hallows Parish Church, where Robert and Anne had married. Anne's home was near the Nene Valley and the bells seemed to peel louder and louder, echoing in the garden and even the house. The bells seemed to reverberate in her head.

Suddenly life all seemed so desolate. Anne could see stretching before her, a lifetime of loneliness. She had only felt hostility from those around her. She began to sob and sob. She couldn't stop. Her mother got angry. "What good is that?" she cried, but Anne just sat sobbing. Her body was wracked with shock and grief. She too had thought that her life with Robert was so good.

She had been at Leicester Training College at 18 studying to be a teacher, when there was a Valentine's Dance. The university had sent a bus with students to the dance and it was there that Anne had met Robert. He danced every dance with her and they agreed to meet again. He had seemed courteous and cultured. They had met for tennis and after nine months had got engaged. During their time together he had no other girlfriend and it had seemed natural that when he finished his degree and obtained the job in Coventry, that Anne too would also obtain a teaching position there.

Robert had suggested they marry and had found the lovely furnished flat. Their honeymoon had gone well. Where had it all gone wrong?

There had been the hiccup with Joan, but it had seemed fleeting. Both only children, they had done everything together since meeting. Now she was alone.

Anne had truly thought life was good. She thought they both loved their detached house with its lovely garden. She had her job as Deputy Head and she did so enjoy it. Robert had started to study part time for a PhD before his firm packed up. Now everything seemed to be in ashes. She could not stop sobbing.

Howard, Anne's father, was concerned. "We must get the doctor," he said.

"Don't be ridiculous," retorted his wife.

Anne carried on sobbing. Her mother was getting more agitated and this brought Anne back to reality. She had to get back to Kenilworth for school tomorrow and she could sense her mother's irritation.

"I'm going home," she said.

"I will come with you," comforted her father. "You can't be alone in this state."

"Yes, go with her and leave me!" her mother suddenly screeched. Her nerves were obviously very much on edge.

Anne knew that her mother loved her father, and had always been a little jealous of the father-daughter relationship.

"If you go, what shall I do?" her mother cried. "When are you coming back? Everything is upside down and it's all her fault. Why did this have to happen to me?"

"To me," thought Anne. "I thought it was happening to me." A steely resolve now set in.

"Don't worry," she said. "I will go on my own and be quite ok."

"Are you sure?" worried her dad.

"Oh yes. I have got it out of my system now, don't worry."

So saying, Anne got into her car and drove back to Kenilworth. It was about forty miles, but the time passed quickly. She suddenly felt stronger, and more resolute.

Chapter 5

When she got back home, she found it hard going into an empty house. The rooms seemed to echo with loneliness. She sensed Robert in every room.

"I think I will get a dog for company," she mused. After school on Monday she went to a pet shop in Coventry. There in a cage was a black rough-coated dog with big brown eyes. The pet shop owner seemed pleased to get him gone. Anne bought the dog a collar, a lead and some food for him.

"I shall call him Beresford," she decided. That evening it had begun to snow and on the way home from Coventry to Kenilworth the little red Spitfire she drove had a job to do the journey on the ungritted road. Beresford sat quietly on the seat beside her. She had no idea how old he was. He seemed fairly big and of indiscriminate breed. When in the house he immediately did a poo and wee in the kitchen, so obviously was not trained.

Such was the state of her mind that she hadn't thought of what was to happen to him when she went to school. Only one thing to do – "I will take him with me," she decided. Which she did. The Headmaster amazingly said nothing, but the children in her class were delighted. The toilet problem persisted, however. Anne's father was a policeman, but very keen on shooting. They had had a dog which sadly had died, when she was ten years old. Her father had trained it to fetch pheasants and the rabbits that he had shot.

"I must take it to Wellingborough," she thought. "And get Dad to train him."

On the Saturday, Robert turned up as promised. Anne had booked 'Hamlet' at the Shakespeare Theatre in Stratford and Beresford was left behind. At the theatre Robert was remote and wooden. He had expressed mild interest in Beresford, but was otherwise really disinterested in hearing about anything Anne had done.

After the play Robert drove back to Kenilworth, but hardly spoke. The snow had fortunately melted. He once again went to the phone upstairs and Anne could hear him laughing. It seemed hopeless. She got the keys of the Ford Zephyr that he drove, but had bought between them, and dropped them in the lavatory cistern.

"I am going back," Robert said. "I have to go to a party. Where are the keys to the car?"

"Gone," said Anne.

Robert said nothing. He patted Beresford, put his coat back on and just walked out. It was quite a walk to a bus stop, but he just went, leaving the car on the drive. Anne realised that all was indeed irrevocable, but probably had really known this from seeing the first note. She had been clutching at straws. She realised that Robert really was shaking the dust from his feet and the only possible outcome was a divorce. He had made no request for furniture or fittings – only taking what he had done on the first day of leaving. He obviously wanted to leave this life behind with no strings attached.

Anne phoned her parents and told them that Robert had left without the car, and then told them about Beresford.

She thought of Robert walking a mile to the bus stop and then having to get a train to London. She had hoped that without the car he would remain – but he hadn't missed a beat. No argument, nothing. He had just upped and gone. She couldn't feel sorry for him, as he had seemed so upbeat in the telephone call – certainly not the sound of a man having a nervous breakdown, something he had claimed. Laughing and joking as if he hadn't a care in the world.

CHAPTER 6

On Sunday Anne drove the Zephyr to Wellingborough with Beresford. As predicted, her mother was not too pleased to see the dog. In fairness, her mother had grown to love Pat, her childhood dog, and Father's shooting companion, but now everything was different. She had a daughter without a husband. Her own husband was worrying about someone else, albeit her daughter, and now there was a dog.

"Can you train him, Daddy?" pleaded Anne. "He doesn't seem very bright and keeps doing poos and wees everywhere."

"I'll do my best," said her father.

Anne had a big bag of dog food with her which of course she left. In fairness, her mother was a good cook and they had a good Sunday dinner.

"I will find a good solicitor," offered her mother suddenly. "You will obviously need to get a divorce."

The year was 1969 and divorce was still mainly for the rich and famous. Never in a million years had Anne ever thought this would happen to her. Robert had always seemed so quiet and steady, but does anyone ever really know anyone? Robert at 22 had been obviously too young for marriage and had not found his feet in life. He was now beginning to take off. Boring domesticity was not for him. London life beckoned with parties and clubs and excitement.

Anne decided that life with Robert was over. She left Beresford reluctantly, but knew that he was safe with her father.

She decided on her way back from Wellingborough to put an advert in the Coventry Telegraph for a companion. After school on Monday, this she did.

An old friend, Joan, telephoned her and Anne told her the sad story. Joan immediately invited her to stay with her husband and herself at Nuneaton for the next weekend. Anne was glad Robert wasn't coming again. Nothing had been said and there was no further communication.

At the weekend, Anne had a pleasant time with Joan and her husband. Anne was grateful for their quiet support and was invited to stay until Monday morning when she drove straight to school.

To her surprise when she got home at night the paper had sent on several letters inviting her to reply. One was from a widower, Mr Simpson, and she phoned him and agreed to meet. She went to his house in Coventry, which was a large semi-detached.

"My wife died after a car accident," he said. "I feel lonely and am in need of companionship."

"Well my husband has just left me and I too am feeling lonely," said Anne.

Mr Simpson was tall and thin, but said he suffered from diabetes type 1. This seemed to make him very pale and Anne did not feel any attraction whatsoever. He was, however, obviously a gentleman. He made no sexual advances and they just talked. He had two children who were away at school. Anne agreed to meet him the next night after school. They went into the countryside and had chicken in the basket at a roadside inn. Mr Simpson was good company and Anne warmed to him. He offered to take her to her parents on Saturday. Glad of something to do, to fill an empty day, she agreed.

On Saturday, Mr Simpson, George, picked her up from Kenilworth. During the journey Anne began to feel nervous.

Her mother's reaction to George was unpredictable.

"I will just go in and see them," said Anne. "And perhaps you would wait outside."

George was a kindly soul and agreed.

Anne went inside. "Just a flying visit," she said.

Her mother seemed quiet. "Your father is ill in bed," she said.

"What's the matter?" asked Anne worriedly.

"I have something to tell you," said her mother.

"What is it?"

"He's shot your dog."

Anne couldn't speak. Her mother carried on. "The dog was driving me mad. I couldn't cope with it."

"Where is it?"

"In the shed."

Anne went outside. Her parents didn't own a car but had had a kind of garage erected next to the house. She opened the door. On the floor lay Beresford, quite dead. Anne was choked. She went inside and went up to her father. He was in bed and looked ill.

"She nagged and nagged. I couldn't stand it. She said she hated the dog. I had to do it."

Anne realised that it was the dreadful deed that had made her father ill. She squeezed his hand and said nothing. Anne went down to her mother. Her mother looked at her anxiously.

"I can't believe it," said Anne. "But I wanted to see you. A friend has given me a lift and I must go."

Anne left quickly. How many more things could go wrong? To shoot a dog! But she knew that her mother had a sharp tongue and she loved her father. She never mentioned the dog to them again. She presumed it got buried in the garden, as her father seemed to recover quite quickly and this he would do. No pet's cremation. It was done and

Anne blamed herself for buying the dog and taking it to Wellingborough. All part of the sorry saga.

Anne didn't even tell George about the dog because she felt so shamed and ashamed. They carried on seeing each other, going for rides in the country, but just as friends. Anne didn't feel ready for anything else, and George seemed very respectful knowing she was a Deputy Head and probably thought things would develop when the time was right.

He did take her to some relations for tea and it seemed that his family were wealthy, owning woollen mills in the north. The relations (Anne never quite worked out who they were), were very polite and friendly. They probably thought she was to be the next Mrs Simpson and George mentioned that his late wife's engagement ring was in the bank!

Suddenly, however, he started to complain of a sore throat and then stated that the doctor said he had throat cancer. Anne was very sorry, of course, but she had not felt any emotional involvement with him. Anne still went for rides with him as he was having treatment for his throat and a date had been set for an operation.

CHAPTER 7

L ife at school went on, but now divorce papers were coming from Robert's solicitor. Her 'crime' apparently was to be 'too dedicated to school'.

All the neighbours at Kenilworth were still a puzzle. They hardly spoke to Anne now and the teachers at school also seemed insubordinate. They had seen her advert in the Coventry Telegraph, and although there was no address, had worked out that it was from her. She found them giggling and sneering about it.

Her saving grace was the children. Every day in the classroom was a joy, and no one mentioned Beresford.

Before Robert left, Anne had been taking the Church Choir as part of her job. Before the disastrous events, she had been training them for a qualification and preparing for a ceremonial Bell Service. After the bombshell, however, Anne had to tell the Vicar she really couldn't do this anymore and luckily the lady she had supplanted was only too willing to take over again. That was another fallout from the saga.

George had sensed Anne's lack of great interest and with his throat concerns seemed to fade off the scene. Anne later learned that luckily he had recovered his health, and married another lady he met through an advertisement. She had sold her flat and moved into his house. She heard that they were very happy.

CHAPTER 8

One of the children in her class was named William. Mr Roberts told Anne that William's father had confided in him that his mother had left home and to ensure that all was well in school. Anne did ask William how he was and William seemed quite cheerful.

"Aunty June is looking after us," he said.

Anne watched him closely, but William seemed his normal happy self.

After a few weeks, Anne went home from school, weary and sad. The phone rang and to Anne's amazement it was William's father.

"I have just heard from a neighbour that your husband has left you. I am so sorry and hope it doesn't affect your relationship with the children. I know how much you care for them. My wife has left me, and I wonder if we could commiserate with each other. Could we meet?"

Anne had met Jeremy St Clare at parents' meetings. He always seemed very quiet and rather remote. Other parents in the past had joked and flirted with her but he had never spoken. The Headmaster had encouraged a 'science making equipment' evening, which as a carpenter he had attended. But he had never spoken to her beyond formality. Anne was surprised to hear from him, but was feeling especially lonely.

"How about meeting me tonight?" she said.

Jeremy replied, "Certainly. How about the Crown and Anchor in Coventry at eight o'clock?"

"I'll be there," said Anne.

Anne dressed in a long black coat and black brimmed hat. "Almost like a funeral," she thought. Off she went in the Zephyr. Robert had not communicated or mentioned the car again. The only communication was now through solicitors.

At the Crown and Anchor, no Jeremy St Clare. Anne bought herself a Vodka and Lime and waited. At about 8.15pm in he came. He smiled at her, noticed she had a drink and went to the bar for an orange juice. They faced each other across the pub table.

"I was so sorry to hear your news," he said. "My neighbour Jill Mackintosh seemed to think it was funny and kept laughing, but I know you do a good job and worried it may affect your teaching. How are you?"

"I was shattered," admitted Anne. "But I gathered from Mr Roberts that your wife had left home. He asked me to check on William in the class, but he seems his usual self. He said his Aunty June was stepping into the breach."

"She did," said Jeremy. "But that all went wrong. She had a row with her boyfriend which threw her off kilter and she left. They actually smashed my dressing table mirror in their argument."

The two of them began to share experiences, and as Jeremy had no car, Anne offered to drive him home. Jeremy had two photographs in his pocket and when Anne got to his house and the car stopped, he showed them to her.

"These are my two boys," he said. "William, you know, and Anthony also in your school but in a younger class." The boys were dressed in Scottish outfits and apparently had been dressed thus for a family wedding.

"That is a lovely photograph," Anne volunteered. "They are both lovely looking boys. You must be so proud of them."

"I am of course," admitted Jeremy. "When Christine left, I told her she would not take the boys."

"What happened exactly?" asked Anne.

"Christine kept coming home late from her work as a receptionist in a hotel. She had offers of lifts and I think she kept the guys talking in the car. I began to wonder what was going on."

"What time did she finish work?" asked Anne.

"About eleven."

"Well surely it was better for her to have a lift safely home."

"It happened too often. She got in at 11.30pm and I lost my temper. I banged my fist into the fireplace and said I had had enough. She just ran out of the house down to her mother and father's house. They didn't live too far away. I don't want her back. She left and that's it."

"Where is Christine now?" asked Anne.

"Oh ho! She quickly moved in with a boyfriend in Coventry's area for Housing Association. I shall definitely never have her back. She could go off again."

"You seemed so happy," said Anne. "I saw you together when you came to pick up the children. She is a lovely looking lady. Why don't you try to make up? You say you lost your temper. Perhaps you frightened her?"

"Well," stated Jeremy. "Something else. My next door neighbour said she had had a miscarriage and Christine said nothing to me. Probably not mine."

"Of course it was," cried Anne. "And that's why she got particularly upset. It must be very, very upsetting to have a miscarriage."

"Something else," added Jeremy. "She did come knocking at the door. She said she would come back if there was no sex. I told her that was definitely a no-no."

"Oh dear," said Anne. "You may have made it up. It all seems so sad to me."

"Well, you can talk," replied Jeremy. "Your husband has left you."

"But no children are involved," retorted Anne. "And talking of children. Look at the time. It's past midnight. Where are your children?"

"In bed I hope," stated Jeremy.

"On their own. I thought perhaps tonight they were with their mother."

"I told you. She is not having them. I asked Amy next door to look in on them. She had a key."

"But they are too young to be in the house on their own. I'm sorry I didn't know. You must go in," said Anne.

"I suppose so. I have to be up for work at 7am. Shall I see you tomorrow?" asked Jeremy.

"I would like that. But what about the children?" enquired Anne.

"I'll ask Amy to look after them. I heard you lived at Kenilworth – your address is in the phone book. I'll get a bus and be there at eight."

"Well, I have enjoyed talking to you," said Anne. "I'll see you tomorrow. Goodnight."

Anne watched Jeremy leave. He got out of the car and walked into his house. It was a bay windowed end terrace. Not too far from the school at which Anne worked. She drove home, thinking as she drove.

Jeremy had always seemed so quiet at PTA meetings. As said, he had never even given her a second glance. His wife was really quite beautiful and always had a lovely smile. A huge dog was always with them. Where was that? Had Jeremy St Clare really got a temper? Enough to drive his wife in fear from the house? What was so wrong with workers at the hotel giving her a lift home late at night? It could be dangerous catching a bus and walking. He had obviously been very jealous. If he had a temper, would he lose it with her? Did he really not want his wife back? All these questions went through Anne's mind. When back home she went straight to bed. She too had to be at school by 8.30am. Still musing over the evening, she fell asleep.

The next evening at eight o'clock, Jeremy arrived.

"What's happening to the children?" asked Anne.

"Oh, they're ok with Amy, the neighbour," replied Jeremy.

Jeremy came into the house and seemed impressed. Anne did not have modern furnishings but had a more classic style. She made coffee and had prepared some sandwiches. Once again they talked and Anne told Jeremy the story of coming home and finding Robert gone.

"I had heard that your husband was a womaniser," informed Jeremy. "Obviously you were known through the school and one of my mates was doing some carpentry at his firm and heard some people talking in the office. That is, of course, before the firm packed up."

"It could just be gossip," said Anne. "But for him to actually leave, it was a shock to me. The good news is that my mother has promised I will not lose the house. She says she will pay off the mortgage and if necessary pay off Robert. My crime, according to Robert's solicitor, is that I was too dedicated to school."

"You are known for that," retorted Jeremy. "And that's what I was worried about, that the worry could affect your teaching."

"It won't," said Anne. "I really love my job. William as you know is in my class. He is a lovely, lively boy and very good at drama. I have to do an assembly every week, so put on a small play with a moral theme. I only have to tell the story and William can act it out with others using his own words. He is quite gifted."

Jeremy smiled. "They are both good boys," he said, "but Anthony is only seven, and William ten. Christine had not even asked for them. I said she couldn't have them, but I still thought she might want to take one at least."

"Perhaps you were so emphatic she didn't dare say anything," argued Anne.

They stayed chatting, no kisses, no love making. Then Jeremy said he must go.

"Let me run you back home," offered Anne.

"No, I'm fine," said Jeremy. "How about going to the cinema on Saturday? I'll meet you outside the Odeon at seven." So saying, Jeremy left.

Anne was tired. She cleared away the cups and plates, and took herself off to bed.

CHAPTER 9

On Saturday at 11am, Robert appeared. "Have you got all the divorce papers from my solicitor?" he asked.

"Yes," replied Anne. "My mother is finding me a solicitor in Northampton. He will get in touch with yours. I have given her the papers. There is no point in your coming anymore," said Anne. "It only hurts me, knowing that you are still with Marilyn."

Robert had driven to Kenilworth and Anne noticed that he had a blue Cortina. "Have you managed to buy a car?" enquired Anne. "We obviously now have separate bank accounts and I suppose your salary goes into that."

"No, it's a firm's car," responded Robert. He made no offer of money to Anne, neither did he mention the house or furniture. It was not discussed.

"What happened to the dog?" Robert asked suddenly.

"My father shot it," replied Anne sadly.

As ever, Robert seemed disinterested and just wanted to leave. Anne couldn't really understand why he had come anyway.

"I want to keep a foot in the door," stated Robert as he was leaving.

Anne was glad to see him go. He seemed to have changed already. He was carrying a little plaid bag – goodness knows what was in it, sandwiches maybe. He looked pale and haggard. He still had a repeated tic in his cheek and he looked uncared for. Still, it was his choice.

"Goodbye," said Robert as if meaning forever.

Anne did not reply. He drove off in his blue car. It did look very second hand, firm's car or not. It certainly wasn't new and looked rather scruffy. Anne's two cars now were on the drive. The Spitfire and the Zephyr.

On the spur of the moment, as Robert left, Anne drove the Spitfire to a local garage. She sold it quickly for far less than they had paid for it, and got the bus back home. "One less thing to worry about," she thought and even though she hadn't received much for the car it was something to live on.

Quite a busy day so far. Anne got into the Zephyr, which still seemed big after the Spitfire, and drove into Kenilworth. There was a lovely little boutique there and she bought herself two suits, one in red and one in purple. "I'm not quite down and out yet," she said to herself. "Robert never liked me buying anything for myself and now I can." She pondered that Robert had never really commented on anything that she wore.

Anne also remembered a dispute in Coventry, when she had seen a lovely cream musquash coat in a furrier's window. It was going for sale very cheaply as the shop was shutting down and fur was definitely out of fashion. As they had a joint account, Anne asked if she could buy it.

"You don't want that," Robert had said. "It would make you look ridiculous." Now she could buy what she wanted, if she had sufficient money of course.

Anne took the two suits home and decided to wear the red one for the outing that evening.

When Anne reached the cinema, Jeremy was outside. The film was 'Far From the Madding Crowd' based on Thomas Hardy's book.

Anne gave Jeremy her share of the cost of the cinema seats.

Jeremy took it and smiled wryly. "I'm sorry," he said, "but thank you. Money is too tight at the moment as Christine has left a lot of debts."

"What are they?" enquired Anne.

"Well she liked nice clothes. Designer clothes. And she got them from catalogues. There are still outstanding bills."

"Your wife always looked well dressed," said Anne.

"But now I have to bear the cost," retorted Jeremy.

"Are the boys ok?" asked Anne.

"Oh they're fine," dismissed Jeremy.

They both enjoyed the film and talked about it as Anne drove Jeremy home afterwards. They stayed in the car talking.

Despite all that had happened, Anne thought she would make a last ditch attempt to reconcile with Robert.

"I am going to Carshalton next week," said Anne. "I am still going to have one last talk with Robert."

"Do what you must," retorted Jeremy. "Can't you sort it out on the phone?"

"He doesn't answer," said Anne. "But my mother has spoken to his father and told him that he was living with Marilyn. His father has made him go back home, as he doesn't want him sued for adultery."

"Sounds a bit odd to me," said Jeremy. "He leaves Kenilworth and then goes back to his home."

"I think he's a bit afraid of his father," stated Anne. "There never seems to have been much rapport between them."

They continued to talk outside Jeremy's house until two in the morning.

"I must leave," said Anne, "or I shall fall asleep."

"Well, when are you going to Carshalton?"

"After school on Friday," said Anne.

They said goodnight and Anne drove back to Kenilworth.

CHAPTER 10

On Sunday Anne phoned Robert's mother and said that she was coming down on Friday night.

"We don't want you here," said Elsie, Robert's mother. "Robert says you have made his life a misery."

"Well now he has mainly moved back to you, I have to really finalise things. I know we have started divorce proceedings, but I was surprised when Harold told my mother that he had moved in with you."

"He has," admitted Elsie. "But he is upsetting Harold. He is coming in at all hours. Harold is afraid to tell him off in case he leaves and we never see him again. Alright, come down, and see if you can talk some sense into him."

On Friday, after school, Anne drove to the station and caught the train to Carshalton. When she got to the house, Robert was there. Elsie put on a simple meal, but the talk was stilted.

Robert and Anne went into the bedroom they had always shared in the house. Robert said nothing, did nothing and Anne soon fell asleep.

When Anne awoke, Robert was up and sitting on the edge of the bed, fully dressed. "I am going out for the day with Marilyn," he said.

"But we haven't talked or discussed anything," said Anne.

"Your mother told my father that she was paying off the mortgage at Kenilworth. You can have my share. I will sign it away. I know it's my fault and I have been bad, so keep the lot. The divorce will carry on though. I promised Marilyn I would take her out today, so I'm going."

So saying, Robert left the bedroom and just seemed to vanish.

It was embarrassing to be left in the house with Harold and Elsie. Anne quickly got dressed, and told them she was leaving. Harold kindly offered to drive her to the station and waited until she got on the train.

They just said "Goodbye" and that was it.

On the journey home, Anne couldn't believe that Robert had been so cruel, to leave her alone with his parents. He seemed to have changed into a different person.

When she got home it all seemed too much. Was she really such a dreadful person? Harold had told her mother that his son had told him she was impossible to live with.

But they had friends. Robert had had a Herring sailing boat for some time (he had bought it without Anne's knowledge and it had just appeared in the garage), and they had taken it out on the Stratford River with friends, Joan and Paul, that Anne had made at her previous school in Coventry, and had later been so kind to her.

They had been ice skating with David, who also lived in Kenilworth. He and his wife Jill only lived a few doors away. David owned a nursery and that is where they really met. They used to go ice skating together in Birmingham once a week and they also went out for meals together. Robert had joined the boat club at the Queen Mother Reservoir so had had space. Had it all really been so bad?

Anne began to sink into depression. She didn't want to do anything back at the house. On Monday she felt that she didn't want to live anymore. She phoned the school and said she was ill. She began to think how she could end her life. What was the point of living? Then she thought of Jeremy. She knew where he worked, and in desperation telephoned him. She asked to speak to Jeremy St Clare and said it was very urgent. Quite quickly Jeremy came on the telephone. Anne was hysterical. "I want to die," she said. "Robert has told his parents that I am a dreadful person; perhaps I am. I think I am going to take an overdose."

Jeremy spoke calmly. "Do nothing, I will come to you. Make yourself a cup of tea. I am coming."

Anne just sat in a daze. All her life seemed to be crashing down. She had been doing quite well. She was comforted that her mother was sorting the house and the lawyers, but suddenly that seemed unimportant. Robert's total rejection suddenly seemed to hit home like a volcanic eruption. Everything seemed as if in ashes.

She took a couple of painkillers and looked at the rest. How many would it take? Would she just fall asleep and not wake? She thought ruefully of Hamlet. She had gained distinction in her 'O' levels in English Literature. The words 'Per chance to dream' floated into her mind from Hamlet.

Before she knew it, there was a knock at her door. There was Jeremy and his boss. His boss had driven him from work. They both talked to Anne. Jeremy stressed to Anne how important her work was with the children. Did she not love that? Had she thought of her mother and father? Jeremy put his arm round her and told her not to give up. "We all have troubles," he said.

Anne thought of him – alone with two young children and began to feel ashamed. She realised with horror what she had done. To fetch him from work with his boss. Common sense roared in.

"I'm so sorry," Anne said. "I will go back to school this afternoon; I have been very selfish and stupid."

Both men stayed for a while until they were convinced she was ok. Anne promised to drive to school. The two painkillers had done nothing, of course.

"I will ring you this evening," promised Jeremy. They left. Anne felt so grateful that Jeremy had come. He had his own troubles and was really, she felt, desperately grieving himself over the fact that his wife was no longer in his home. She realised that he had loved his wife desperately. Probably too much if that is possible, as he had obviously been insane with jealousy. Anne realised he could not have deep feelings for her, but perhaps there could be a response to a mutual need for comfort and maybe some caring.

Anne did pull herself together and went to school in the afternoon. And that evening Jeremy telephoned.

"Shall I come over?" he asked.

"Yes please," replied Anne.

She was still not really herself and didn't think how he was going to get to her. She didn't even know the time when Jeremy did come. She made him a coffee and again she apologised for being so stupid and causing such a fuss. She realised that Jeremy's boss must hold him in high regard to bring him to her house.

Jeremy passed it over and just stayed chatting about his work and life in general. Anne again offered to run him home, which she did, but she asked about the children and then remembered that he had had a dog. She asked about its welfare.

"I couldn't leave it in the house now that Christine isn't there. She was there in the day for the children and took the job in the evening as we needed the money. But with me out all day until 5pm and the children at school, I have had to have him put down."

Anne was upset. It sounded a similar scenario to her father shooting Beresford. She realised that there were similarities in personality between Jeremy and her father. Jeremy had obviously got a strong personality, as had her father. Her father also had a temper and had had many clashes with her mother.

Although she was a little shocked, she could understand that he couldn't keep a large dog now. "But," she wondered, "couldn't it have been re-homed, or sent to the RSPCA or something?"

As she had been such a nuisance that day, she decided to let it go. Nothing she could do now, but it made her realise with Jeremy's temper causing Christine to leave, and now letting his dog be put to sleep, he was in fact quite a strong character.

They stayed talking in the car, however, and the time passed. Suddenly Anne heard a milk cart. "Goodness," she said. "It's five o'clock and we haven't had any sleep. I must go."

"How about we go for a ride on Saturday?" said Jeremy.

"Where to?" asked Anne.

"Down south somewhere."

"What about the children?"

"Oh, I'll let their mother have them."

"Ok. I'll pick you up at ten o'clock."

So saying, Anne drove off, got home, and just managed a couple of hours' sleep before going to school.

CHAPTER 11

The week went well. Whether William knew that she was now friendly with his father, Anne was unsure. He had a lovely personality and was so good at acting in her School Assembly day, which was always on a Tuesday. He was always the central character in her moral play which was of course fairly short, but held the whole thing together with his ability to ad lib.

When Saturday came, Anne drove over and picked up Jeremy. She wasn't quite sure where to drive, but headed south. She carried on to Bournemouth and they just had a teacake and a coffee in a small café by the beach. They sat on the sand and just talked about anything and everything.

Anne was a bit surprised when he mentioned that he could put his house in trust for the boys. She wondered if he was seriously considering moving into her house with his children. It was very early in the relationship, and with her job she didn't feel ready to cope with two young boys, lovely as they were. William was super, but very boisterous and Kevin was obviously pining for his mother. She decided to say nothing, but a warning light flashed in her brain. Was she being courted for her possessions, she wondered? Did Jeremy want to leave his house and mortgage to come into the large house that she owned? His comment did not sit well with her.

"We must be getting back," said Anne. "But the weather has been fine and the sea lovely. It seems a shame to go, but go we must."

Anne had obviously parked the car in a nearby car park to which they returned and they set off for home. It was now getting late and about nine o'clock. Suddenly the car shuddered to a halt and a head of steam seemed to come from the area of the bonnet. Anne lifted the bonnet lid and a jet of steam and smoke poured out. She tried to start the car again, but it was hopeless. Anne had learned a bit about cars, although she had not passed her driving test until she was 26. Her priority after getting married had been to save for a house. They had had a semi-detached house firstly in Coventry but no car. Anne's mother had lent them the money then for a car and then Anne had driving lessons and passed the first time. The first house had been sold to put the deposit down on their lovely house in Kenilworth. They had of course also repaid the money that Elizabeth had lent them for the car. They then had a Ford Anglia, but that soon got changed for a Classic, then a Cortina and then of course the Zephyr that was now puffing smoke by the wayside in Andover. Anne realised that they were marooned, at now nearly 10 o'clock at night. Spotting a nearby hotel, and leaving Jeremy totally perplexed sitting in the car, she went into the hotel and asked if they had a vacancy.

"We have a double room available," said the receptionist.

"Fine," said Anne. "We have broken down and cannot get home. We will take it." Signing the register, Anne then went back to the car which luckily was near a layby. They managed to push it off the road and Anne told Jeremy what she had done.

"There's no choice," she said. "I'll have to find a garage in the morning if there's one available."

They went into the hotel and were shown to their room. A double bed! They had no nightclothes, so after making a cup of tea and having biscuits in the room – obviously too late for a meal, Anne had a shower, then put her underslip back on. Jeremy did the same, but kept his underwear on and so into bed.

"I have some condoms in my pocket," offered Jeremy.

Anne was speechless. Why would he have those? Never had he made any improper move nor indicated that he was interested in a sexual relationship. She knew that he had two children, of course, but that was with the wife she realised he had loved and must really still do. "Did she really know this man?" she thought. They had met as two lost souls, desperate for some comfort and company, but this was taking things to a new level. The irony was that Robert had never seemed very interested in sex. They had not had sex before marriage, but the honeymoon had been fine. Robert used to say 'A bit of alright', but that was only for a week. When they had returned from their honeymoon, back to their flat, Robert didn't seem to appear too keen. On one occasion when Anne had suggested sex – not Robert initiating it – he had said, "Oh must you."

Jeremy put his arm around Anne, and began to stroke her. Anne kissed him; they began to cuddle. Jeremy went and got the condoms from his pocket and put one on. He tried to make love to her, but then suddenly laughed. "I can't," he said, "I just can't."

Anne was secretly relieved because she still felt unsure in the relationship; circumstances had thrown them together that night, and she realised that Jeremy was still hurting from the break up with his wife. Anne had been thinking 'if Robert can have Marilyn, what is sauce for the gander can be sauce for the goose'.

Jeremy seemed quite unruffled. He still kept his arm round Anne and they fell asleep.

The next day they had breakfast but then there was the problem of paying the bill. Anne did not have her cheque book with her and at this time debit and credit cards were not in fashion. The year was 1969.

Anne scrabbled in her bag for money and Jeremy too had very little with him. But they scraped together enough for the bill and asked if there was anyone in Andover who could help them with the car. Luckily the receptionist had a brother who had a small garage and she said she would ring him and ask him to help. And help he did. He managed to tow the car to his workshop, but said it would take all day to fix it.

Luckily the weather was fine, so Jeremy and Anne walked for miles around Andover. They sat in a bus shelter and talked. They managed to buy a coffee and some toast with the little money they had left and then returned to the workshop at 4 o'clock. To Anne's joy the car was fixed. It was indeed the head gasket that had blown. It had not been filled with water (Anne didn't understand this) and that had been that.

"It will be £200," said the guy.

Jeremy looked blank.

"We haven't got it with us," Anne said. "But I am an honourable person. I am a Deputy Head of a school and will send the money as soon as we get back. We just didn't expect this to happen and so grateful to you for doing the work."

"I don't think I can let you have the car," said the mechanic whose name was Bob.

Anne had a ring on her finger given to her by her godmother. "Look," she said, "this ring is valuable. I will leave it with you as a pledge that I will send the money."

"How will you get the ring back?" asked Bob.

Anne was so desperate she hadn't really thought about that. "I could send you the postage for recorded delivery and a thick envelope," she suggested.

"This is getting too complicated," uttered Bob, obviously rather annoyed. "Give me your address. I shall have to trust you. Take the car. Here's my card so that you can send the money."

Thanking him profusely, Anne and Jeremy got into the car.

"Phew," thought Anne, "what a catastrophe that was."

CHAPTER 12

Anne drove back and they were fairly silent. Jeremy was concerned that Christine had returned the children to an empty house. They had expected to be back on Saturday night. Anne was worried whether the car really would make the journey back. It did and Anne waited outside Jeremy's house to hear about the children.

"They're not here," said Jeremy after going inside. "I am going to ring Christine and see if Barry, her boyfriend, will bring them back. You go home and get ready for school tomorrow. We are lucky to have got out of that disaster."

"I am so sorry," said Anne. "I don't really know about looking after cars. I always left that to Robert." Anne actually felt like crying. Everything always seemed to be her fault.

"Don't worry," said Jeremy. "Come round tomorrow night about six. I'll give the boys a sandwich when I get in from work and then I'll cook something."

Anne didn't know that he could cook, but she felt too distraught and weary to question this.

"Fine," she said. "Again, I'm so sorry." So saying she drove home.

She did have a lot of questions on her mind, but she still got out her cheque book, wrote the cheque for Bob, or rather Robert Marks, and put it into an envelope using the address on the card that he had given her, and posted this immediately in the nearby post box. She returned home and made a cup of coffee, had a biscuit and phoned her parents.

She told them of the saga, but missed out the bit about one bedroom. Her father was upset but glad that it was sorted. Her mother did ask if she was ok for money and Anne told her that their savings in the Coventry Building Society had been unfrozen for some time. Robert had made no withdrawals from this and she had her salary always paid into her own account at Barclays. She knew if necessary her mother would have helped her, but she was in some ways now enjoying her independence with money. She remembered how Robert had not wanted her to have the musquash coat, but had ordered and paid for the boat from their joint account, without telling her.

The boat was still in the garage and Robert had not mentioned it. It was as if he just wanted a new life and was prepared to leave everything, money, house and furniture behind as if it had all never happened.

She pondered about Jeremy. She had been startled when he said he had condoms in his pocket. Were they there really for her? She was obviously not naïve, but it had all seemed just sort of chummy, and she had thought that he was still looking at her as the Deputy Head of his son's school. "I suppose men are men," she mused. But what about his comment about putting his house in trust for the boys? She hadn't liked that at all. She carried on with her thoughts.

"Why had Robert always seemed so disinterested in sex, but now indisputably in a sexual relationship with Marilyn?" Anne was certainly human. She had received two offers of marriage at 17 when Secretary of the Young Conservatives in Wellingborough. That was before college. No boys had ever gone further than kissing her, however, and from her upbringing she was content with that.

The next evening, Anne didn't drive back to Kenilworth after school. She had taken the girls for shinty, a kind of hockey/netball with shinty sticks and a hard ball. It was played on a netball court. There was a Shinty Association and she was a keen member. After practice and seeing the girls out, she drove round to Jeremy's house. There was no garage or drive, so she just parked outside as before after driving Jeremy to his home.

She knocked tentatively at the door and Jeremy invited her in. She went through a narrow hall into a dining room. The children were apparently in their room upstairs. She hadn't known what to expect, but the furniture was the old G Plan type in light wood. The one thing that really jarred on her was surprisingly the carpet. It had triangles of bright red, bright green and yellow, with black edging. Nothing was to her taste. There were two wooden armchairs as well as the dining suite, so Anne sat down. Jeremy had gone into the kitchen. Something crackled as she sat down so she lifted the cushion. Under the cushion, to her amazement, were copies of Playboy magazine, with some rather dubious pictures. She stuffed them back hastily.

Another conundrum. She had never imagined that the serious, quiet Mr St Clare that she had seen at PTA meetings would read such literature, if that is what you could call it.

She began to feel a bit uncomfortable. It was rather embarrassing being in the home of the pupils. She also felt awkward that Jeremy was cooking. He came in, put place mats on the table and cutlery.

"Meal's ready, boys!" he called. Down they scampered. William smiled and sat down. Anthony was very shy and didn't look at her.

Jeremy brought in two plates at a time and put them down on the table. Anne too sat at the table and looked at her plate. There was just some mashed potato, some mushy peas and some brown things. Anne had never seen them in her life.

"What are these?" she asked.

"Oh faggots," said Jeremy. "We have them a lot."

Anne ate her food silently. The boys too were quiet.

"Have you had a good day?" Jeremy asked William.

William glanced at Anne. They had had a usual day in class – Arithmetic, Nature Study, PE and Composition. William had written that when he grew up, he wanted to be a soldier.

"William wrote a good composition," Anne volunteered, as William hadn't replied. "The subject was, 'What I think I would like to do when I grow up', and William wrote an excellent composition about wishing to be a soldier."

"At the next school, Blue Coats, they have a cadet centre. Maybe William could take part in that," volunteered Jeremy.

"That would be great," said William.

They finished the meal quickly. There was no pudding.

"Go and play in your room," said Jeremy as he collected the plates.

Anne went into the kitchen to help wash up. It was narrow with a cooker and washing machine, but no dishwasher. "The washing machine isn't working," stated Jeremy. "I don't know what's wrong with it. I'm taking the washing to the launderette."

Anne could see that they were struggling. After washing up, Jeremy took her into his front room. That had a large bobbly brown suite with a huge settee, a small television and again she was aware of the carpet. This time, splodges of green, black and white.

They sat down and Jeremy talked about his work at Bittswell Aerodrome – mainly as a carpenter. He said he was only paid if he got there and his dread was missing the bus in the morning which left at 7.30am, nearly opposite his house. It was a works bus and if he missed it then he lost a day's money.

This was all a new world to Anne. Her teaching salary was paid every month and before that she had been supported by her parents. Her mother had a successful shoe business and, as said, her father was a police officer. There had always been plenty of food in the home which had antiques from Howard's family home. Lovely furniture they had had as wedding presents and Elizabeth had bought some excellent pieces from Jeffreys of Northampton. There was Dresden and silver in the home.

Of course, Anne and Robert had started out in a furnished flat, but for their first house Elizabeth had soon organised Queen Anne furniture and given Anne a Kemble Minx Pianoforte. Anne and Robert had soon acquired some silver for themselves from antique shops in Wannock, and this was added to by Elizabeth, Anne's mother.

Anne could see that money was tight with Jeremy. Christine had had her children when young and didn't seem to have had any help from her family whom Anne knew were actually quite comfortably off. Anne had learned that Jeremy's parents were in Council Property and had little money.

None of these things really mattered to Anne, however. She had a companion with whom she could share her troubles and he had been kind enough to invite her to his home.

"Why don't you stay the night?" suggested Jeremy.

Anne thought "Oh!" and then thought did she really want to do the lonely drive back to Kenilworth. She wasn't prepared to stay – no nightdress or pyjamas. She was feeling rather apprehensive. "What about the children?" she said. How would this play out with William in her class.

"I have to give them their breakfast early now, before I go to work, then they stay in their room before school. They have school dinners, of course. You can just pop out and drive to school. I'll bring you a cup of tea and biscuit before I go."

Anne wavered. What had she got to lose? Only her parents seemed to care about her and inside she still felt broken.

"Thank you," she answered.

The boys stayed in their room and Anne went upstairs. The bathroom was nice. Traditional black and white tiles and a white bath with black sides. Black and white checked floor, but all clean.

The bedroom was not so good. The dressing table mirror was broken. The cupboard doors were padded with black squared material and the long table by the bay window was unvarnished. However, there was a cosy inset gas fire and that cheered her.

Jeremy had nylon pyjamas, but again Anne only had her underskirt. Not knowing what to expect, Anne got into bed. Jeremy seemed tired. Once again he put his arm around Anne and they fell asleep.

Before Anne knew it, Jeremy was up, dressed, there with tea and biscuits and said, "Come again tonight."

"I must go back to Kenilworth," replied Anne.

"Well come later then," answered Jeremy.

Looking ahead at a life of loneliness, Anne agreed.

CHAPTER 13

When she did get to school, William was exactly as he had always been. No sly looks, no nudges to his classmates, just a model pupil as before. "He is a lovely boy," thought Anne. "How can his mother bear to be without him?"

The next night Anne didn't get to the house until 9.30. The children were in bed. This time of course she had a nightdress with her, but once again Jeremy only put his arm around her. This pattern carried on for the week. Divorce letters were still coming from Robert's solicitors. They were very incisive, completely exonerating Robert from any blame. It all seemed rather a waste of time, as Elizabeth was completely paying off the mortgage and Robert was relinquishing any claim on house or furniture.

Anne was surprised when at home to get a phone call from Robert's mother, Elsie. "I have called to ask why are you taking so much money from Robert," she said.

Anne was flabbergasted. "I'm sorry, I don't know what you mean. Robert left £20 when he left me. The accounts were frozen as he had the books, but that is sorted. There were little savings and now I have my own Barclays account. We split the little savings we had. Robert has not given nor is giving me any money at all."

"Well, he doesn't seem to have any money. He says he is giving it to you."

"That is not true. I am living on my own salary that is paid into the bank. My mother is paying my solicitor's fees but I am managing by myself. Does he not give you anything for when he is with you?"

"No, nothing. He must be spending it on that girl. Harold is worried about him. He comes in sometimes in the early hours of the morning and upsets the household. Harold is still afraid to say anything, in case he goes away for good."

"Well, I'm sorry about that, but I can assure you that he is not sending me any money."

"Oh well – goodbye."

So saying, Elsie put the phone down.

Anne knew that Robert was getting a good salary from London Computer Service, and wondered what he was doing with his money. He must be wining and dining Marilyn, she thought.

Elsie must be feeling very strongly about the situation to pick up the phone. She was a clever but neurotic woman and for her to phone was very unusual.

On Saturday Jeremy showed his temper, the temper that had driven Christine away for the first time. Anne believed the children were with Christine, and Jeremy had arranged to come to Kenilworth on the Saturday evening by public transport.

They had a pleasant time and were just talking when suddenly Jeremy said: "I'm going."

"But you have only been here an hour," protested Anne.

Jeremy didn't say it nicely, but said curtly, "I'm going."

He didn't give Anne a chance to say "Let me drive you home". He just walked out. Anne's heart sank. It was pouring with rain. Torrential. He was storming up the road. Anne ran after him.

"Please don't go like this," she pleaded. He took no notice and carried on. She still ran after him in the pouring rain. "Please come back," she begged. "I will run you home." She had to beg several times, before he agreed to come back, so that she could run him home.

When she ran him home, the children were still with Barry and Christine. Barry was going to bring them back on Sunday morning.

Jeremy was in a foul mood. Quite different to the quiet person of before. However, he made a cup of tea and suggested they go to bed.

In the morning she drove back to Kenilworth. Had she said something to upset him? She tried to remember what they had been saying, but couldn't think of anything that could have provoked the sudden swing of mood.

He told her that the children were with Barry and Christine and he must have suddenly thought of that and got upset. Anne realised that she had a problem with him, but her fear of loneliness led her to let it go.

She went to her parents on the Sunday and had a lovely Sunday dinner. Her mother was a great cook. She told them all about Jeremy and the boys, but missed out the bit about Jeremy's sudden temper.

She was now getting used to going home into an empty house. That had been hard at first, but she did not mind driving home alone. "I suppose you get used to things," she thought.

The next night, after school, to her amazement, Jeremy arrived at her house at about 7 o'clock. "The neighbour is looking after the boys," he said.

No apology. Anne too did not refer to the incident, but secretly felt humiliated. Running after him in the rain, what had she come to. A sad and desperate woman. She realised that she had been quite cocooned. An only child, not spoiled, but wanting for nothing. Friends at school and college and then Robert. She had never really had to be totally alone. The fear of this was now evident in her behaviour.

For the first time Jeremy kissed and caressed her and Anne was pathetically grateful. Almost like a wounded puppy searching for affection.

Jeremy suddenly said, "If you get a piece of paper, I will write (when we are free), that I will marry you."

Anne wasn't sure if it was a joke. She got paper and pen from the bureau and Jeremy wrote simply: "I, Jeremy St Clare promise to marry Anne Deighton when it is possible," signed Jeremy St Clare.

Anne smiled and put the paper in the bureau. She did wonder at the imbalance. She had reasonably well off parents, a good secure job, a detached house nicely furnished. Mirrored tables, chandeliers and silver. Japanese plates on the wall. Sheepskin rugs on the Wilton carpet, a large car and still a boat in the garage. Was Jeremy hoping to move in? She remembered again his previous remark about 'the trust for the boys'.

The thoughts trickled through her brain, but she put them to one side. She was a cast-off wife and that was a fact. She was hurting still and probably even now in disbelief at the hand life had come up with. Her pride was salvaged a little by the fact that someone had offered to marry her if free. She let Jeremy carry on kissing and cuddling her. She guessed that probably he was an expert lover. However, he had to get back home. Putting out the lights and locking up, she took him home and stayed.

Yes, Jeremy was an expert lover. After Robert's lack of interest and the "Oh must you," she felt cherished and desirable.

Anne was slim and her mother had actually said to her when she was seventeen "You are flat chested. Men like something more"! Anne repeated this to Jeremy who laughed and said, "More than a handful is too much."

CHAPTER 14

The next day Anne went to school with stars in her eyes. She was wanted. Someone wanted her. Good riddance to Robert. She still went back to Kenilworth after school. Her mother had told her to enjoy her home. To lie in the pink bath in the bathroom and to think that Robert was going from some sort of flat to his mother's house, whilst she could still enjoy the comfort of the Kenilworth house. This she did and began to feel that life was not so bad until she went to school that day.

The Headmaster sent for her at playtime. In his office was the Attendance and Welfare Officer. "We have received a complaint," he said. The Attendance Officer Mr Elgar looked very uncomfortable. "There is a letter from a Mrs Palmer, she says you are coming from Jeremy St Clare's house to this school. She is concerned that this is not a good moral attitude for a Deputy Head."

Anne had heard of Mrs Palmer. She was divorced with one daughter at the school, but not in Anne's class. Anne knew that the Headmaster was delighted with this. He had not chosen her as his Deputy, but wanted Mrs Bireham on his staff. Anne didn't know what to say. It was true. She could not deny it.

"Yes, I am friendly with Mr St Clare," she stated. "But we are both separated from our partners and the friendship is fairly recent."

"I can see no wrong in this," spluttered Mr Elgar. "I feel that the letter is written out of malice; Mrs Palmer is on her own and she may be resentful. Perhaps she would have liked to be friendly with Mr St Clare."

The Headmaster turned rather red and said grumpily, "Well go and have your coffee, Mrs Deighton."

Anne escaped. Mrs Palmer did live near to Jeremy and probably had a hopeful eye on him. "Who knows," she thought. Still, it was very unpleasant. But what was wrong? They were both separated and both getting a divorce. Jeremy had contacted a 'free' lawyer and Christine was not contesting it. She too was apparently making no immediate claim to the house or contents, and Jeremy was paying the mortgage.

Anne still felt a surge of resentment that Robert had thrust her into these situations. She had thought her life so fine before Robert left, now the problems kept mounting.

After school, Anne went to Jeremy's house. The children were having their tea and Jeremy was home. Anne never left school early, either doing sports with the children, or putting up work in the classroom. At present she had ships made by her class hanging from the ceiling.

She asked Jeremy if he could talk to her and they went into the front room. She told him about Mrs Palmer's letter and her summonsing to the Head's study.

"I do know Mrs Palmer," admitted Jeremy. "She has been on her own quite a while. When Christine left she called and offered her sympathy. I thanked her, asked her how she was doing and that was that. I did have the feeling that she would have liked to stay longer and maybe hoped for more, but I showed her out fairly quickly. She didn't seem genuinely sorry about Christine and in fact said 'Your wife always seemed to have a lot of new clothes, I expect you spoiled her.' I wasn't in the mood for that."

Anne decided to go back to Kenilworth and still felt sad and hurt. It was a difficult situation with Jeremy's children in the school. Did she really want to be involved with a man with two children? They could never be fully hers as their mother was still alive and of course loved them. Was it right for children to be without their mothers? Jeremy was obviously trying to do his best, but nothing could replace a real mother's love.

She didn't go back to the house that night and stayed away for the rest of the week.

On Saturday she mowed the large lawn as it was now growing. Jeremy appeared at the back door. "Let's go for a drive," he suggested.

Anne made him tea, quickly changed and thought perhaps she would drive to a country pub for something like 'chicken in a basket'. She assumed the children were with Christine, but didn't ask.

As they were still driving on the main road, and they were talking, Anne could not remember afterwards what they were talking about. Jeremy suddenly banged his hand on the dashboard and said, "Stop the car." Anne was startled and put her foot on the brake. Bang! The car behind went into them. Jeremy just opened the door, jumped out and ran off. Anne had to apologise to the driver behind who luckily had hardly a mark on his vehicle, which was actually a large van.

They exchanged insurance details, but the driver, having no obvious damage, was unconcerned. He was, however, puzzled at a bloke rushing out of the car. He said, "That bloke's a fool. Are you alright?"

Anne thanked him for his concern and drove on to Kenilworth and went to a local garage. There was a dent in the bumper but they said they would fix it over the weekend. Anne said she would not claim on the insurance, but would pay them immediately. They kindly ran her back home and

Anne again felt shattered. Why had Jeremy rushed off? Why had he banged the dashboard? She could only guess that he was suddenly missing his children, but it was not her fault. He hadn't suggested that they should be with them. Anne went back to her gardening.

On Sunday she stayed in bed for a long time. She did some housework, but there was only dusting to do. Later the car was returned to her quite ok. Anne wrote a cheque and breathed a sigh of relief. She watched the television in the evening and the next day went to school as usual.

CHAPTER 15

After the day at school, Anne decided to go to Jeremy's house. She did some marking and put up some work in the classroom. Perhaps she had said something to annoy him, but she had never come across such behaviour before. She didn't like the lonely abyss that stretched before her.

She drove round to his house when she knew they would all be in and knocked on the door. Silence. She thought she could hear a scuffling so knocked again. Nothing. She knew that the boys would be in, so guessed they were being silenced. Sadly, she walked away. She certainly wasn't going to ring up and beg.

The next day after school she drove into Coventry. After the disaster with Beresford, she thought she would buy a kitten. Back to the pet shop she went and there in a large cage was a small orange coloured cat with blue eyes. The poor thing was only £15. She bought some more milk and tuna, and didn't even know if it was a boy or girl. The pet shop owner didn't seem to know and seemed only too glad to get rid of it.

Anne had also bought a carry cage to take it home in. "I shall call you Marmalade," she thought. She was fairly sure that Marmalade was a tom cat, but it was pretty. When she got back to Kenilworth, she gave Marmalade its meal. It was so small and seemed to want to scamper everywhere. She took Marmalade to school with her the next day. When she told the staff its name, one member, Miss Brodie, sneered "What an original name". Some of the staff still seemed to think that she was a pariah, because her husband had left her.

She had taken Marmalade in his carry cage into the classroom, but there was a very big cupboard in her classroom, large enough for anyone to sleep in. It was a walk-in cupboard with shelves for exercise books, stationery, paints and papers. There was plenty of floor space for Marmalade, and Anne had milk for him. At playtime, of course, the children played with him and also at lunch time.

When back home Anne was careful to keep him in the house, but he was so small she didn't think he would venture out. From items in the garage, she made up a litter tray. He had obviously had a few 'accidents' in her stock cupboard, but she had cleared this up.

Marmalade went to school with her the next day. The children were delighted and took it in turns to play with him where possible. Amazingly the Headmaster, who had got to hear, again said nothing.

That evening there was going to be a PTA Social for all the parents. It had been arranged for some time and was to be held in the school hall. The School Secretary, a tall, bony woman with glasses, who moaned about doing it but refused to give up the job, organised the refreshments in the school passage. Although it was organised by the PTA, Anne guessed the money came from the School Fund to pay for the sandwiches, tea and coffee.

Anne went home to Kenilworth with Marmalade and changed into a white lace dress with long sleeves. Although she was only 34, she remembered going to Birmingham months ago with Robert and when she had bought it he had sneered, "It's a bit young for you isn't it?" He was going to London at the time, and she had not realised that it was a warning sign. The beginning of the end.

Back to school with Marmalade. There was music for dancing organised by the PTA. The music was fairly sedate –

waltzes and quicksteps. As the hall filled, she put Marmalade into her classroom with the door shut. He still had some milk and had had his tuna. Couples began to dance. As Deputy, she greeted people and anyone not dancing, made them feel welcome.

As she stood in the hall the Headmaster walked by. She knew for sure that he wouldn't ask her to dance – which he didn't.

Then, to her surprise Jeremy appeared. He smiled and winked at her.

"I have a kitten," said Anne. "In my classroom."

"Let's have a look," he offered. Jeremy found Marmalade and gave him a cuddle. "Anthony would just love him," he stated. "Why don't you come back afterwards and show it to the boys?"

"Are they on their own?" asked Anne.

"The neighbours are babysitting."

"The kitten is called Marmalade," said Anne.

"Well, you and Marmalade come back afterwards. I'll wait for you if there is some clearing up to do. Anyway, can I help?"

Anne realised that an olive branch was being offered, but really wanted to know why he had lost his temper and why he hadn't answered the door.

She helped serve the refreshments and take coffee to the PTA members who were also busy. The hall was quite full and everyone seemed to be enjoying themselves. Anne loved dancing, but no-one asked her if she would care to dance.

It ended at 1am. The parents left and the PTA soon cleared up. Collecting Marmalade, Anne went to her car. Jeremy was there.

"You can drive me back." He smiled.

Anne did just that. They went into the house with Marmalade who, when out of his carry cage, promptly ran up the curtains in the front room. Jeremy thanked the neighbour and called the children down from upstairs although it was late. They were both delighted with the kitten who suddenly seemed to want to race everywhere.

They also got milk for Marmalade. Jeremy had an enclosed conservatory at the rear of the house. "Marmalade will be quite safe there," he offered. Anne realised for sure now that she was to spend the night at the house.

After a while Marmalade was put in the conservatory and the children went to bed. Again, Anne had no nightclothes. Upstairs they went and once again Jeremy made love to her gently and then slept with his arm around her. Anne was too tired to analyse anything and fell asleep.

Before Jeremy left for work the next day, he said, "Shall we all go to Bournemouth on Saturday?"

It was a long drive, but Anne had nothing else to do. "Very well," she said.

"I'll see you tonight," Jeremy offered as he left.

The week went on but what to do with Marmalade if they were all driving to Bournemouth? It was the sweetest kitten, but, like Beresford, it had been a rather selfish impulse buy.

The next day in class she told the children that she needed someone to look after the kitten for the weekend. One boy, Alexander, offered at once. "I would love to," he stated, "and my parents will be fine. I'll bring him back to school on Monday."

Anne made a decision. "If you wish to keep him, you may," she said. "If you don't wish to keep him, just return him. If you wish to keep him, I shall not mention it again."

After school, Anne put Marmalade in his carry cage. Anne loved the kitten already, but knew she couldn't take him to Bournemouth on Saturday, and it was difficult to look after the kitten. Alexander kept the kitten.

CHAPTER 16

On Saturday they drove off. It was a long way, a six-hour journey. They had started at ten and arrived at four o'clock after making a couple of stops on the way for the toilet and Anne bought them all some refreshments. She realised that Jeremy would have little spare money.

When they got there, Anne parked the car and they went onto the beach. But the children didn't seem to know what to do. They went to a local café and Jeremy paid for the boys, but Anne gave him the money for herself with which to pay.

Five o'clock. Anne realised that they would be home late. It had been too far to travel there and back in one day. She began to get a migraine.

"I can drive back," offered Jeremy.

"Can you?" retorted Anne.

"I was in the National Service, and went abroad. I learned to drive then and have kept up a provisional licence."

Anne felt that somehow it was breaking rules, but her head was splitting. She wasn't fit to drive.

When they got to the car, she handed Jeremy the keys. She was past caring as she felt so ill.

Jeremy got in the driving seat with William in the passenger seat. The back seat was large and Anthony was quite small. She just curled up in the space with her head throbbing. Jeremy expertly manoeuvred the car out of the car park and drove home. Anne's head hurt so much she was hardly aware of the journey.

They arrived back amazingly at 10pm. The boys had a drink and went to bed. Anne was past caring, she just undressed and got into the bed and fell asleep. She had known that a provisional driver should have 'L' plates and a qualified driver should sit beside them. "Goodness knows what would have happened if stopped by the police," she thought in the morning, but Jeremy seemed so confident, and appeared a good driver.

In the morning, Anne still felt unwell and stayed at the house until late morning. Jeremy fed the boys and made her some tea.

"I'm going to book a driving test," he informed her. I did plenty of driving abroad so there will be no problem."

Anne was again surprised with him, but stated that she must get back to Kenilworth.

"Perhaps we can go to Bournemouth again next Saturday," suggested Jeremy.

"I'm sorry," replied Anne. "It is too far. I cannot do it again after a week at school."

Again Anne saw a flash of temper on Jeremy's face. "If you say so," he retorted quite crossly.

Anne drove back home. She now felt better back on home territory. She phoned her parents and then went to mow the lawn. It was a big garden and she noticed to her horror that the dividing fence was down between her garden and the next. This was the house of a sneery neighbour. They hadn't been there very long and she had not even seen his wife.

She went round and knocked at the door of the neighbour. She didn't even know his name! He came to the door.

"Why is the fence down?" asked Anne.

"I'm going to creosote it."

"But it's my fence."

"Well one panel was loose and I am helping you."

"Did you need to take it down?"

"It looked shaky to me. I'll do it as soon as I can." So saying he shut the door.

Anne felt that she was being taken advantage of. Why take the whole fence down? Anne phoned Jeremy.

"I have wood preservative. I'll come and put it up. I'll bring the boys with me."

Anne forgot to ask how they were coming. She was so used to having a car, but Jeremy's neighbour drove him over with the children. They were happy to play in the garden as Anne mowed the lawn. There was quite a large patio for them to play on.

Without a word to the neighbour, Jeremy soon re-erected the fence and coated it on Anne's side with more preservative. It had been done previously when erected at the time the house was built. The neighbour said nothing. He did not even appear.

Robert would have been too afraid to do that, and Anne thought it was quite good to have a strong man with her. Jeremy was tall – about six foot one – but Robert had been the same height as herself, five foot eight and a quarter inches and certainly had never liked confrontation. The fence was back up, looking better than ever.

Anne gave them all sandwiches, a drink and then drove them back to Coventry. It was now about seven o'clock, so once again Anne stayed the night. Guessing she would stay, she had thrown some things into a holdall. Once again, Jeremy made love to her and Anne began to feel more married than she ever had with Robert. She was so grateful that he had erected the fence, that she mentally forgave him for the other mishaps – to which she did not refer.

Chapter 17

Anne had decided to change her car. The Ford Zephyr was really too big to drive into the Coventry car parks. Ford had brought out a new Ford Capri and Anne received notification that the white one she had ordered was in. She told Jeremy that she was going to change the car and it could be collected on the Saturday. The garage were doing a part exchange. Jeremy suddenly seemed furious.

"I like the big car," he stated. "Why do you need to change it?"

"Well, it is rather big for me to drive around," she replied. "I cashed in my Spitfire after Robert left. I only got the Zephyr after hiding the key from Robert in the beginning when he visited, so that he wouldn't leave. But he still did. My own car was the Spitfire."

"The Zephyr is better for my boys to travel in, "retorted Jeremy. "I have told my family that I am driving it."

It seemed to Anne as if Jeremy had been bragging. "What have I got to brag about," she thought. Jeremy may have thought that he had stopped Anne from getting the Capri, but whilst Jeremy was playing football for his firm, Anne went to the garage, paid the balance (she had cashed in a small savings account that Robert had completely forgotten about but as he paid her nothing she had no conscience), and drove away in the Capri. Strangely enough it did seem small after the Zephyr.

That evening she drove round to Jeremy's house. He saw the car out of the front room window and said nothing, but looked very annoyed.

"I have the Capri," volunteered Anne.

"So I see," replied Jeremy. "I don't know what you paid for it, but it doesn't look worth much. I'm taking my test next week and have an old banger in mind. Still, why should I worry. I don't need a new car. You have a new car and a big house, and they are almost mine."

Anne was shocked. She knew that Jeremy didn't love her. She had seen too many signs in his temper. But to be so blatant, she could hardly speak. Things got worse. It was obvious that Jeremy was furious that she had bought a smaller car. He had obviously felt very important driving the Zephyr. He carried on, "If we live in your house at Kenilworth, I can drive to work from there. You could take the boys to school."

Anne made no answer. It was lonely at Kenilworth, but did she want Jeremy and two boys at her home? She was dedicated to her job, but could she cope with two boys? Her house at Kenilworth was immaculate – toys, friends, comings and goings. It was not her lifestyle. She did love children, but Robert had not seemed interested – well, he hadn't seemed interested in sex at all, and that was the irony of it all.

Anne didn't know what to think. Jeremy had made no concessions such as 'My share of the house could come to you'. Just a complete take over. There was no 'should we' or 'could we'.

Again she felt plunged into sadness that Robert had somehow jettisoned her into this predicament. Jeremy seemed to be using her as a stepping stone to a better life. But was it a better life for her? The boys were lovely, but William was indeed boisterous as you would expect in a boy of that age. Anthony was very quiet and did appear rather resentful, but he was younger and really needed his mother full time.

Christine was their mother. She loved them and of course they loved her. What possible chance did Anne have in this situation?

She nursed her hurt and still said nothing. Jeremy obviously noticed her reticence and his face had set as in stone. Anne drove back to Kenilworth from an atmosphere of icy silence as Jeremy was still sulking.

That night Anne drove to Jeremy's house and once again there was no answer. As this had happened before, Anne just drove home. She was still upset and confused. She didn't want to be on her own again. The neighbours at Kenilworth were still not speaking to her and it still seemed as if she had committed some crime. They probably felt embarrassed, but there were no commiserations and no offers of help. It was now fast growing time for the lawn and Anne mowed the entire garden herself after school. She went to the nursery and put in the bedding plants. The garden was looking lovely.

After a few days she returned to Jeremy's house. It was pouring with rain and outside his house was a white car. She knocked on the door and Jeremy let her in.

"I've passed my test," he said. "It was on Monday, but I kept it quiet in case I failed. I didn't think I would, but you never know."

"Congratulations," Anne enthused. "That's great."

"And I've got the car outside cheaply from an old work mate."

"Well done," continued Anne. "That's wonderful. I'll have a good look at it."

They both went outside. The children were in their room and it was approaching dusk. Anne could see a row of small studs along the side of the car.

"What are they?" she asked.

"What?" said Jeremy.

"These little studs."

"Oh no! They are rivets. I saw the car and bought it cheaply, but didn't see these. It was raining and I couldn't see them."

Jeremy went into the house and put his head in his hands. "I should have waited and bought something better."

"You've passed your test, that's the main thing."

"I've rushed into this. The bloke that sold it to me is a mate. I can't take it back."

"Well, if it drives alright, don't worry."

Jeremy seemed to plunge into despair. Like Anne, he too was still rocked by the break-up of his marriage and his life. Anne realised again that they were both still suffering from the chaos caused by their partners leaving them. Anne had never seen a man cry. Her father was a very strong personality – that is probably why she could withstand Jeremy – but he had never ever cried. Jeremy wasn't actually crying, but he still had his head in his hands in total despair.

Anne stayed the night and comforted him. Once again, he put his arm around her and she too felt some comfort.

CHAPTER 18

The school was building up towards the School Fete. They had stalls run by parents for grocery and bric-a-brac. Always, Jeremy, before Anne was friendly with him, had run the 'Throw the Wellington' or 'The crockery stall'. At this, crockery was stacked up and people paid to throw balls at it. It always seemed a bit destructive to Anne, but people seemed happy to do it.

As usual Anne went round to Jeremy's house after she had been to Kenilworth. She didn't get there until nine o'clock.

"You're late," stated Jeremy.

"I've been doing the gardening," replied Anne.

"Oh! And who are you doing it for? Just to impress the neighbours I should think."

"No. I do it for myself," uttered Anne.

Suddenly Jeremy seemed to turn on her.

"You only want your garden to look nice for the neighbours to see," retorted Jeremy again angrily. "There must be better things you could do with your time. Why come here so late? What have you really been doing?"

"I have mowed the lawns," answered Anne. "Swept up. Did some dusting inside. I didn't leave school until 6 o'clock."

"Well that doesn't help me," said Jeremy angrily. "Why should I help you and the school with the Fete? I am going to tell Mr George I am not going to help at the fete."

Jeremy seemed to be behaving totally irrationally. Against all logic.

"What has the fete got to do with anything," Anne thought.

To her horror, Jeremy was looking in the telephone directory, then made a phone call – obviously to the Headmaster.

"Hello, Jeremy St Clare here. I am not going to help at the School Fete due to the behaviour of your Deputy Head. Why should I help you when she is so selfish? Goodnight." Jeremy hung up.

Anne was appalled. She could not believe that he had done that. To jeopardise her job was beneath contempt. She would not and could never do such a thing. She just looked at Jeremy aghast. What on earth would happen when she went into school the next day? The Headmaster resented her as it was. She felt too drained to drive home so went upstairs and got into the bed. Neither of them spoke.

The next day the Headmaster pounced. "I don't know what you are doing involving the school into your private life. Mr St Clare is now not helping at the fete. What have you done to so upset him? I was always doubtful at having you as my Deputy and you are bringing the school into disgrace."

Anne was mortified. She knew that it was only the Vicar who had wanted her as Deputy because she could play the organ and originally trained the choir.

At lunchtime she went up to The Vicarage and saw the Vicar. Suddenly she couldn't stop crying. It was all too much. She sobbed out some of the story, but had to say how very hostile the Headmaster had always been. She sobbed and sobbed but the Vicar was very discomfited and did not know what to say. Anne felt that he had been of no help whatsoever, so she thanked him for his time and said that she had to get back as lunchtime was nearly over. She managed to drive back and once into her classroom she felt herself again. Whether the Vicar had said anything to the Headmaster she did not know, but the matter of the School Fete with Jeremy's phone call, was never again referred to.

But what about Jeremy? There were so many things now stacked up against him. She spoke frequently to her parents on the phone but could not tell them of this or other things he had done. Her father would be furious and think her mad to continue with the relationship. But could she exist all alone at Kenilworth, forty miles from her parents? It seemed childish, but as said before, she had never really been alone. She had built her life around Robert. Holidays at his parents' home, holidays with Robert and her parents. Who else could she meet with whom to be friendly?

Having no pride, Anne drove back to Coventry. Jeremy let her in and neither referred to the previous evening. A knock came to the door and Jeremy went to answer it. The children were in the front room where they had been watching the TV. Anne was sitting in an armchair.

Jeremy came in. "It's Christine," he said. His face was ashen. Christine came in and sat down. Anne was paralysed. What should she do? Should she leave? She couldn't offer her tea in her own house. Christine was so lovely. So gentle. But Anne couldn't really hear what she was saying. She didn't give a reason for coming and Anne was completely at a loss. Christine seemed to be talking about the next school for William, the Blue Coats which was still a Church school. Jeremy sat as if frozen and answered in monosyllables. Later Anne thought that she should have left the room herself, but instead said, as a way of escape, "Shall I put the children to bed?" thinking this would leave Jeremy and Christine alone.

"No," barked Jeremy.

Anne subsided into the chair.

"Well, I only popped in to say that I wanted the boys to go to Blue Coats," Christine volunteered and got up to go. She smiled at the boys and Jeremy saw her out.

Anne felt dreadful. How sad that she couldn't or wouldn't stay, but she knew that she was now living with this guy called Barry in this housing development area. She was still working at the Leofric Hotel. The children seemed strangely unperturbed by their mother's visit and went to bed upstairs by themselves.

Anne could see that Jeremy looked shattered. Now that Christine was living with Barry it was all too late for any reconciliation, but it was clear that he probably wished that he could turn back the clock.

Once again, Anne made excuses for him in her mind. Two of the cleaners at the school lived in the same road as Jeremy and knew all of the story. Gossip spreads rapidly. They had talked to Anne after school one day and she had confided some of her hurts to them.

"He's using you as a whipping boy," one of them said.

Anne realised this to be true. He was resentful if they went out on their own without the boys and lashed out at her verbally to ease his own unhappiness.

Once again, they went to bed in silence, deep in their own thoughts, but Jeremy still put his arm around her.

CHAPTER 19

The day came for the School Fete. The parents were all busy in the morning (Saturday) setting up stalls and organising refreshments. What would Jeremy do? Anne was helping the parents together with the rest of the staff. Anne saw Jeremy go onto the far side of the field and put down some markers for 'Throw the Wellington boot'. It was a strange game, but if the markers were hit, you got a return of money. Not the crockery smash, however. Nothing was said and as broken crockery was brought in by some parents and no one seemed to be organising it as a stall, another father just set it up and organised it. Jeremy just stayed out in the far corner of the field.

The weather was fine and the day went well until the Headmaster appeared to be on the wrong end of a discussion with a parent. Anne went over to see if she could help. The parent, Mr Hill, was red in the face. "The Headmaster wants me to have an audit for the Bingo I run on Wednesday," he stuttered. "I charge admittance and I get the prizes. I refuse to run it if there is to be an audit. I do it for the parents of the school, not for myself."

"We are very grateful," said the Headmaster. "But there should be an audit."

"I refuse to do it then," shouted the father. "And I'm taking my son away from this school. Other parents will join me. You are being high handed. The PTA is to help your school and you are throwing it back into our faces."

Mr Hill stamped off and the Headmaster looked devastated. Anne wondered why he had suddenly demanded an audit. For several weeks now, Mr Hill had run Bingo nights charging admittance in the school hall and obtaining the prizes. Had the Headmaster suddenly become concerned that there was a discrepancy in the admission fees and the cost of the prizes. It had never previously been queried and had started before Anne became the deputy Head.

The Fete drew to an end, but some parents were glaring at the Headmaster. Word had got around.

On Sunday Anne went to visit her parents. She glossed over all the problems with Jeremy and certainly didn't tell her father about Jeremy ringing the Headmaster. She had informed them of her friendship and told them about the two boys. She had relayed that Jeremy was a carpenter, but had fitted kitchens for his bosses at work and had made some very nice small carved chairs. That was the good thing. Jeremy had actually carved a small hall chair for herself, as a peace offering after he had banged out of the car some time ago now. It was very skilfully done with Tudor roses carved into the back.

Her mother was talking of the solicitor's letters passing between her solicitor and Robert's. Robert's solicitor was very good, mainly putting his client in a good light, but there was no argument about the property or furnishings.

When Anne went to school on Monday the Headmaster was in a spin.

"Mr Hill has taken his son out of the school," he informed her, "so have six parents also taken their children away. There will be no more Bingo because Mr Hill will not do it and no one else has offered."

Anne was puzzled how all this could have taken place so quickly. Perhaps the parents had been in touch after the fete or very early on Monday morning.

The Headmaster looked ill. None of the children concerned were in Anne's class so she carried on as usual. The Headmaster came into the staffroom at playtime and told the staff of the problem. He also said that he had had phone calls from parents that morning supporting Mr Hill and complaining that the Bingo was stopping.

The next day the Headmaster was not in school. The message was that he had influenza and would be away for several days. That left Anne in charge, but she still had her class to teach. The secretary answered the phone but the problems regarding the Bingo seemed to suddenly die down once parents realised the Headmaster was not in school.

Anne still went to Jeremy's house in the evenings and after going home to Kenilworth. The house was now definitely in her name as Robert had not reneged on his promise. The final papers had been drawn up and Anne now owned Kenilworth. She couldn't understand why the divorce was taking so long because there was nothing to argue about. Robert had complained that she had been a dreadful wife – obsessed with school – but how many times could you say that? So be it. He was settled with Marilyn sexually but still his residence was his parents' home. His father seemed obsessed that his son should not be not charged with adultery, but what on earth did it matter if Robert so badly wanted a divorce? Presumably he was going to marry Marilyn.

Jeremy seemed to be calming down again. He had his car, but still caught the bus to work.

The Headmaster did not appear, and seemed to be having some sort of breakdown. A dinner had been booked at a hotel for the PTA and payments had already been made. This went ahead on the Friday evening and Anne had to act as hostess to parents. Most of the PTA attended and Jeremy of course was there. Nothing was said about the Bingo, nor the absence of the Headmaster, and actually everyone seemed quite jolly as the meal was good and well served.

Jeremy had come in his own car, and Anne drove back in her car to his house. Again, the neighbour had acted as babysitter. Jeremy suggested that night that they all went on holiday together. They could travel in Anne's car to Bournemouth. Anne thought this a good idea. She and Robert had had some lovely boating holidays at Bournemouth, and stayed many times at some super hotels. Still, that was in the past. Now she booked up into an inexpensive boarding house somewhere in the back streets. They were to go immediately after the break-up from school.

The Headmaster was back at school and things were running normally. Nothing was said by the Church Governors as chaired by the Vicar about some children leaving the school. At least if it was said at a meeting, it was not relayed to her.

It was a lovely summer for weather. Anne took her class out for rounders and took the girls after school for netball. Interestingly, the staff were now very friendly with Anne and one member invited her with a plus one for an evening at her house. Anne went with Jeremy. He was back to his old self, quiet, respectful and full of decorum. He put on a grey suit that he had (probably bought for his wedding) but it still fitted him. He was actually quite handsome, slim as well as tall, and he made Anne feel more feminine. She quite liked the fact that he could be quite masterful. To her, Robert had often been indecisive. She had found their first house and it was she who organised most of the furniture (although they both paid for it) through her mother, who bought it from a good furniture shop in Wellingborough and got it delivered to their house. Her mother had had the curtains made and sent them via delivery van. Robert had appeared quite happy about this. His only decision was to buy the Heron boat. Often Anne had felt more like his mother than his wife.

The evening went well and Jeremy was the perfect escort. Afterwards Anne went back to his house. The same pattern for her emerged. School – Kenilworth –Coventry.

The children had taken to coming into the bedroom and chattering to her after Jeremy had left for work.

The school broke up and the next day was the holiday. Anne did the garden at Kenilworth, dusted and packed. She was late to Jeremy's house and again he was annoyed. She just could not make the decision for them to move into her house and it would have been difficult for Jeremy to get to work or the boys to school.

CHAPTER 20

It was an easy journey and they soon found the Boarding House, The Fairstow. It was larger than she expected. A double room for herself and Jeremy, and a twin bedded room for the boys. They were very happy. Anne had bought them new blue and pink shirts with matching bow ties to go with their blazers. Anne had bought Jeremy some more new shirts and he had purchased a blazer. They seemed a perfect family. The boys settled into their room and Anne began to unpack.

Then disaster struck …

There was a huge wardrobe and Anne was carefully putting her things on two shelves when Jeremy suddenly appeared behind her.

"You are taking up all of the wardrobe," he stated.

"Look, I'm only using these two shelves, there is plenty of room for you."

Jeremy glared at her, turned and ran out of the room. He didn't go to the boys. Anne looked out of the window and saw he was running down the road. Her heart sank. What was she to do? She couldn't run after him. The boys had found the shower – which was separate to their room – undressed, and were having a lovely time splashing water over each other. They sounded so happy so Anne let them play. She carried on unpacking; she didn't have a great deal – underwear, a few dresses, jacket and bathing costume. There was plenty of space left in the wardrobe. She sat in the bedroom and waited. The meal was not until 6.30pm and it was only 5 o'clock. The boys stopped playing and got dressed. They came to find their father and herself.

"Your father's gone out," declared Anne.

The boys said nothing. It seemed as if they were used to his mood swings. Anne decided to take them for the short walk to the sea. They walked down the cliff steps and sat on the sand. People were now leaving the beach for dinner, but some happy souls were still making sandcastles. The sun sparkled on the sea as it just began to go down. A beautiful scene.

They then had a walk along the sand. Anne was thinking, "Where had Jeremy gone? Would he come back?" He had probably run off because she wasn't Christine, but things were different for her too. Now with two children in a Boarding House, albeit a good one.

Hitherto, as stated, she had stayed in four and five starred hotels with Robert and her parents. She had stayed at The Eastcliff, The Carlton and The Haven at Sandbanks. She had made a big effort then to dress for dinner. Now they had both had a change of circumstance. Anne felt the strain of not knowing what to expect next.

They all walked back to the Boarding House. There was Jeremy sitting on a chair outside, casually smoking his pipe as if he hadn't a care in the world. It was time for dinner and in they went. Again, nothing was referred to, the boys chattered happily, wearing their new shirts and bow ties. Anne let the conversation flow normally. The food was excellent, the service excellent. She had chosen a good place.

In the evening they sat in the lounge and watched the television. There were not too many guests and some had gone out.

That night Jeremy again made love to her. Anne felt more at peace with the world.

Each day went well, good breakfasts, paddling and swimming in the sea, long walks and back to the hotel. There was an embarrassing incident on the beach. They were sitting on the sand, Jeremy in his bathing trunks (he must have bought them specially), the boys in theirs (also purchased), and Anne in her bathing suit. Her Uncle Arthur, her father's brother, owned a large factory that made women's wear, and he had always provided Anne with bathing costumes, sent via her mother and father, since she was a toddler.

Two ladies sat beside them. "You are a lovely family," one said. The other said to Anne, "You would never think you had had two children. One is fair though (William) and takes after you and the other dark haired (Anthony) and takes after his father."

William's eyes sparkled mischievously, and he looked at her and smiled. Both boys, well trained in obedience by their father, said nothing. Anne just smiled, Jeremy smiled politely and they moved on. Anne had to credit the boys with tact, as some children would have spoken out, "She's not our Mum!" But no – they remained loyal; Anne was very proud of them.

The holiday went well. No more hiccups and everyone enjoyed the sun, sea, air and the very nice Boarding House. A holiday in the end to remember.

CHAPTER 21

When they did get back to Coventry, Jeremy soon returned to work and Christine sometimes had the boys. At the weekends Jeremy did some outside painting at Kenilworth and they also drove in the countryside. They could not afford to go into hotels or public houses, but took a flask of coffee with them.

The final stage of Anne's divorce was here. Her solicitor had written stating that Robert should finally agree to the divorce and not approach Anne again. To her amazement a letter was returned to her solicitor stating that Robert wished to come to Kenilworth, did not finally agree to the divorce (she thought it was now irretrievable breakdown and not adultery), and wished to see her. The date given was next Saturday. Anne made an excuse to Jeremy and as now as before Robert appeared in a blue Cortina car. He looked smart in a silver grey suit (again probably from their wedding). Anne looked good. Slim in a navy dress and pink sandals. Her Capri car was on the drive. The garden looked lovely.

Robert walked in and sat down. Anne made tea and sandwiches. Robert just sat in the dining room and looked out at the garden.

"I shouldn't have left," he said.

Nothing was said about the divorce, in fact nothing much was said at all. He did say that he and Marilyn had been with some friends camping in France and that they had taken turns at driving. He didn't say whose car or what they drove.

He said that the camp site wasn't too good, and he didn't appear to have enjoyed himself very much. As before, he didn't stay long, but said he thought the house looked lovely. He remarked on what a lovely area Kenilworth was. He was still working at London University Computing Service and still mainly based at his parents' home in Carshalton. He noticed the name of the house (Beaumont) had worn and promised to get another name plate made. It was of carved wood with black lettering, but the varnish had cracked.

Anne thought he looked well, but sad. He said the blue Cortina was a works car. He drove away and said that he would be in touch. She should have told him to keep away. He was still involved with Marilyn and no doubt going back to her. She looked at her options.

To live alone

To be with Jeremy and his children and his moods

Still a chance with Robert.

She decided to do nothing drastic and carry on.

When she went back to Coventry, to her amazement only Jeremy and Anthony were there. "Where is William?" she asked.

"He is more like his mother. I have talked to Christine and she is happy to take him. Anthony is staying with me."

This was all such a shock. To split up the two boys seemed cruel. William did resemble his mother, but it was all done so suddenly. Was William happy about this? What about Anthony who seemed to withdraw more into himself. His playmate had gone. When had all this discussion occurred?

"He's more his mother's boy and Anthony is more like me," offered Jeremy. "I had to laugh when I took William to his mother's house. Barry came to the door. He stepped back as if I was going to punch him."

Anne dared say nothing. She just couldn't believe that he had split up the boys and surely the younger boy should also be with his mother. Maybe more so than William. William was an extrovert, and Anthony an introvert. Jeremy had always seemed so adamant that he keep both boys. When had all this brewed up in his mind?

Anne puzzled further. Did Jeremy hope that she would take one boy and himself? It had never been discussed and was a bolt from the blue. She dared not say that to split the boys was cruel – which of course it was. She did not realise that this was the beginning of a seismic shift. Jeremy almost immediately became very, very possessive of Anthony. She noticed that if she tried to befriend the poor boy, he became jealous, and if she backed off he got nasty. There was now a triangle and she felt the odd one out.

Anne had told her parents, of course, about Jeremy. They had been told that he lived in a terraced house and money was short. They also knew that Anne was lonely and desperate for company. She asked if she could bring Jeremy and Anthony over. She drove them over in the Capri. They arrived for a Sunday lunch. Elizabeth was a wonderful cook, and they had a lovely meal. Jeremy was the perfect gentleman and was happily able to talk about shooting and fishing with Anne's father. Anthony was as usual quite, but beautifully, behaved. After lunch Anne's father offered to take him to Wellingborough Zoo which was open. Off they went. Elizabeth washed up and brought in coffee. She was very tactful when talking to Jeremy. She asked about his work and hobbies and told him about her shop. After Howard retired from the police force and taking on a security job at Sywell Aerodrome, he now helped Elizabeth in the shoe shop that she had taken over some years before. She amused them with tales of the customers, and how some would bring back shoes that had never been bought in her shop.

Howard came back as well with Anthony who looked happy. The zoo was set in the grounds of an old Abbey. It was quite small but had a delightful aviary and some lovely parrots.

It was clear that Elizabeth liked Jeremy. He was at his most charming and not at all reticent. He offered to make Elizabeth a stool chair and she was delighted. Howard showed Jeremy his guns in the gun case upstairs.

After tea it was time to go. Howard said to Anne, "I could trust him to keep you safe anywhere in the world." That was a compliment from her father. Robert was a bit of a coward and ages ago Anne had told her parents how they were tailgated to the house. Robert had run inside, leaving her to deal with a car full of laughing men.

On the way home, however, Jeremy seemed sullen. Anne could only think that it was because she had caring parents and a good home. He was one of four and told her that he had been hungry as a child. His mother had made some soup for his grandmother and he had to carry it to her. On the way he took out all the meaty pieces. His 'crime' was discovered and his mother had hit him several times. His mother had, however, at least got him an apprenticeship as a carpenter, and this had proved invaluable.

Chapter 22

Life carried on and Anthony made no reference to his brother, but it was apparent that father and son were more closely bonded.

One night Anthony was in bed and Jeremy was kissing Anne. Anne sat on his knee and felt her cares drop away. Suddenly the door opened and Anthony appeared. Anne jumped off Jeremy's lap with a gasp. Jeremy turned on her at once.

"Don't frighten the boy with your stupid behaviour."

Anthony looked worried. "I can't sleep," he said.

His father ignored Anne and of course comforted his son. Anne could not intervene and just felt guilty that she may inadvertently have caused the boy any concern.

Anthony went back to bed and Jeremy was back to his moody self.

William was going to his new school Blue Coats in the September and at the weekend Jeremy asked Anne if she would come and help to choose his uniform. She agreed willingly. Jeremy picked William up from his mother and into town they went. They soon found the store that sold Blue Coats uniforms and Jeremy obviously had the money to pay for it. Anne didn't know how much he earned, but they led a simple lifestyle. They did not go out for meals and if they went anywhere Anne paid her share, such as the cinema.

They bought the uniform and William was happy, but Anthony had not had anything. Jeremy was now getting a bit crotchety. They went into another store and Jeremy told Anthony to choose some gloves. Why gloves, Anne didn't know, but perhaps because they were a cheaper item. There were plenty of woollen gloves for sale in all colours. Anthony couldn't make up his mind. Anne went over to help him and Jeremy immediately barked at her, "He doesn't have to have gloves if he doesn't want to."

Anne backed away. Another disaster. Jeremy took William back to his mother and William seemed quite content. Anthony, as usual, was quiet.

Anne stayed at the house and whilst Jeremy and Anthony ate some tea (she didn't feel hungry), she tried to do some housework there. Jeremy was quite organised and the place downstairs was tidy.

The problem was Anthony's bedroom. Now there was an empty bed where William had slept.

"I am going to turn Anthony's room into a sort of study," said Jeremy. "You needn't do anything there because I am going to take out the spare bed and fit shelves, bookcases and a work station."

Anne swept the conservatory and looked at Jeremy's garden. It was dreadful. The grass had grown and was full of weeds. It didn't look as if it had been mowed for months – even years! It was too much for her to tackle. She thought of her lovely garden at Kenilworth. Her parents' garden was large too and of course mowed by her father. She couldn't help wondering what she had got herself into. Was this life really for her.

The first house that she and Robert had bought (on a mortgage of course) had been new. It had a big plot and they had soon grown a lovely lawn and edged it with fir trees. The front garden was similar with rose trees and firs in each corner. It had sold very quickly when they decided to buy the detached house at Kenilworth.

Anne had not heard from Robert and felt in a quandary. Anyway, after viewing the garden really fully for the first time, she realised that Jeremy had little interest in gardens. Maybe in the beginning he couldn't afford to do anything and now had lost complete interest. "Had they anything in common," she thought. "Did she want a man who was no gardener?"

As usual, they went to bed, and Anne felt this was better than being alone at Kenilworth and forgot her concerns.

Anne went back to Kenilworth and did her own garden. She did love it and so loved the environment. Anne phoned her parents and thanked them and they were pleased that she had some social life.

As Robert had not finally signed the divorce papers, they knew that there could be nothing serious in the new relationship. Anne had no plans in her mind for such either. She was concerned with Jeremy's mood swings and realised once more that he did not love her. It was just a friendship for mutual advantage.

Jeremy asked that night when she once again went to the house if his parents and sisters (three) could visit Kenilworth on the following Saturday. Anne didn't like to say 'no' but had some concerns. "What should she give them all to eat?" She knew that Jeremy's father was a retired lorry driver and of course that they lived in a council flat. Jeremy had taken her there briefly, once, at the very beginning of their relationship. His father had not spoken to her, but just watched the TV all the time. She didn't like him at all.

Anyway, Saturday came. Jeremy's sisters were married and had cars. In they trooped. It was as bad as Anne had feared. They picked up the pieces of silver and examined them. They put their fingers all over her gold mirrored tables. They oohed and aahed and said "Ooo our Jeremy," as if he had won the lottery. The sisters' laughs were coarse and Anne was cringing. She served tea and cakes and showed them the rest of the house and garden. Once again she wondered what on earth she had got herself into. The Kemble Minx piano her mother had bought her for her first house was in the main room and Anne played the piano to them. She was a classical pianist so could not play popular music. However, they listened and with more oos and ahs decided to leave after having another good look around. Anne definitely got the impression that they thought this was to be Jeremy's future home. Anthony was not with them but playing at a friend's house.

After waving them all goodbye, Anne felt drained. Jeremy helped to clear up and they went back to Coventry to pick up Anthony.

What an experience!

Anthony had now found a playmate and a neighbour with whom he could have a sleepover. He was going to stay the night there after all, so Jeremy and Anne once again went to the cinema. Anne tried to enjoy the film, but the events of the day still played on her mind.

Jeremy was a good lover and to Anne this was Shangri-la after the reticence of Robert. She wished that his love making translated into the day.

Again on the Sunday she went back home and did some housework and gardening. Robert phoned and said that all was not well with Marilyn. He said that as she came from New Zealand originally, there was a culture difference. Anne couldn't quite understand that. It seemed apparent that things were not going too well. But how could they if Robert was still based at home? That wasn't showing a sign of commitment. It was neither one thing nor the other. Anne could see that he was confused, but he had left home and must have thought it all through beforehand. He had told her he didn't love her, so why wouldn't he just sign the final divorce papers?

That night, at Jeremy's, he suggested that they go on holiday together but this time to go abroad. He said that Anthony could stay with his mother and they could fly from Luton. Anne was all in favour of this adventure and suggested that they go to a travel agent for some brochures. Of course it was Anne that went and Anne that booked it up. She chose Rome, Naples and Pompeii. She paid the deposit, but Jeremy agreed to pay for his share of the trip.

CHAPTER 23

When October came, Anne drove to Luton and they boarded their flight to Rome. The coach took them to their hotel and Jeremy was very happy. They visited the Colosseum and the Pantheon.

A coach then took them to Naples where there was a power cut, but that made it all the more romantic. The coach then took them to Pompeii, where Jeremy was entranced with the archaeological remains and existing frescoes.

The coach took them back to Rome and then to the airport and back home to Luton. It had been a wonderful trip and Anne had really enjoyed Jeremy's company. He was more vocal than Robert and made things appear interesting. Robert had always seemed too quiet – but had Anne ever really known him?

Anne wished the holiday had lasted forever. Jeremy seemed poised and confident. The amusing thing was that when it emerged that one of them was a Deputy Head, other travellers with them assumed that the Deputy Head was Jeremy, and that Anne was a secretary.

The Jeremy on holiday was a dream, and Anne could have lived every minute again. He was kind, considerate and very good company all the time. He too had obviously enjoyed the holiday.

Back at Coventry Jeremy had to pick up Anthony. Anne drove back to Kenilworth. A letter was waiting for her. It was from Robert.

Dear Anne,

I have made a terrible mistake. I am very sorry. I want us to start again. I am coming on Saturday to see you.

Love Robert

A brief cri de coeur. The euphoria that still remained from the holiday with Jeremy quickly went. What to do? Robert had caused so much trouble. Her mother had already paid quite a lot of money in divorce fees with the solicitor. All the upset. The fact that at one point she had felt suicidal and Jeremy and his boss had come and comforted her.

There was a dichotomy. An uphill and down dale life with Jeremy, or her old life back with Robert. But could she ever trust him? He obviously had an eye for other women. She reflected that he had a rather negative personality and a slight inferiority complex. Being with other women made him feel macho and important.

However, old habits die hard. She posted a letter back to say that he could come, but on Sunday.

Sunday came. Jeremy presumed Anne was back at Kenilworth gardening. Robert arrived. He looked very forlorn. He came in and sat down and cried. "I took Marilyn to a dance and she went home with a chap called Michael. I think she had been seeing him for some time. It's all over. Finished." He whimpered.

Anne didn't know what to say. To want to come back to her just because Marilyn had left him was hardly flattering.

"I should never have left. I was having a breakdown doing the journey. Also, I couldn't commit to Marilyn because of you," Robert added.

Anne still had feelings of guilt because she had not encouraged Robert to seek redeployment in the firm. She had wanted to stay at Kenilworth and keep her job as Deputy Head.

"All I've done for that girl, and she just left me at the dance," added Robert.

That bit didn't sound so good. "What do you expect me to do?" enquired Anne.

"Well, you could get a job down south. You could sell the house and buy one near to your new job," said Robert.

This is exactly what Anne had not wanted to do when Robert was made redundant. But perhaps she had been wrong. Had it been fair for him to have to travel to London and back every day? Once again, Anne felt guilty. She was partly to blame as well. She had been obsessed with her job, as Robert's solicitor had mentioned.

"I really don't know," said Anne. "I shall have to think about it." The standard of her old life beckoned. Jeremy was poor and she really couldn't make a breakthrough with Anthony.

When Jeremy was with his son, she felt the outsider. Was this the life she wanted – to be number three? She knew that counsellors would say "Try harder". She had, but Jeremy became so jealous. He obviously had a jealous nature. His son was his son and he made it clear that she was not to interfere. It had been fine just the two of them on holiday, but life was not full of holidays.

Anne was giving in. "I will look for jobs down south," she conceded. "But I cannot promise."

"I've ever only wanted you," urged Robert. "That is the reason it didn't work with Marilyn. She knew that I kept thinking of you."

"Could have fooled me," thought Anne. But still her old way of life beckoned enticingly.

"You know that I have met Jeremy, but things there are not straightforward."

Anne gave Robert some sausage rolls and coffee and he said he would leave her to think about it. He would return next Sunday. He left.

Anne phoned her parents.

"You must be mad to even think of going back to him," her father said angrily. "All we've been through, the divorce nearly finalised. What are you thinking of?"

"I think Jeremy would like to move into Kenilworth with his son, Daddy," Anne stated. "I'm not sure that it is for the right reasons. I liked my old life with Robert. At least he didn't have mood swings and we had a good way of life together."

"You must do what you think best," said her father. "But your mother's brother Tom said he thought Robert was a rotten apple after his behaviour, and in a barrel of apples, the rotten one should be thrown out."

Anne had no answer to this. She knew that her father was concerned for her and indeed he had been a great strength and rock in the whole ordeal.

Anne drove to Jeremy's house and said nothing of Robert's visit. Jeremy seemed upset. Apparently, although he had paid his share of the holiday, he was now worried about the community charge on top of the mortgage. "I think that I may have to ask my parents to move in with me," he volunteered. "They could share in the bills and their pensions would help to pay other expenses."

"Would they do that?" asked Anne.

"Oh I think so. I don't think they particularly like their flat. As you know the area is covered in graffiti, and they don't like being high up."

Anne pondered on this. Selfishly she knew that if his parents moved in, could she still visit. There were three bedrooms, but Anthony had one room, and already when she was at Kenilworth Jeremy had started to build the work station and bookcases promised. He had broken up William's bed and put a worktop there. Then there was Jeremy's large bedroom and a small box room. Where would they sleep? Was this a cunning plan to thrust her into the position of inviting Jeremy and his son to stay with her?

"How much are you in debt?" she asked.

"Well, I need £100, but I'm sure my parents would like to come here. They also have to pay rent and they can pay that to me instead."

Things were getting confusing. Anne had never given Jeremy any money for staying the night. She hadn't even thought about it. Equally when she had driven him around, she had never asked for petrol money.

She made up her mind. After school on Monday she went to the bank and drew out £100. Jeremy was not home. Anthony was home alone, but he let her in. She went upstairs and put the £100 in the box room where he used to change.

She stayed with Anthony until Jeremy came home, then said she must return to Kenilworth. On the way home she stopped at a newsagent and got the most recent Times Educational Supplement.

Back home she scanned the paper for positions down south. There was a Deputy Headship in Tooting and a Headship near to Godalming in Surrey. She spent time applying for both. 'What will be, will be,' she thought.

She posted the applications and drove back to Coventry. Jeremy had found the money.

"Santa Claus has been," he chortled. "That will save the day."

He didn't actually thank her, but seemed happy and did not mention his parents coming again.

CHAPTER 24

A week later she had two letters. Both inviting her for an interview. The first was in Tooting, the second Godalming. She still said nothing to Jeremy. She had to ask the Headmaster, Mr Roberts, for time off for the interviews, which of course he had to grant.

The interviews were on consecutive days. She left Coventry at 8am and was in Tooting in time for the 11 o'clock interview. There were seven candidates. The committee seemed to like her ability to offer music to the school. She was called in after all the interviews and was offered the position. She returned to Coventry, picked up her car from the station and drove to Jeremy's. She still said nothing. Anthony was in the class below hers and hadn't realised she was not at school.

The next day she went to County Hall, Kingston upon Thames, for the second interview. This was for a Headship. There was only one other candidate, the present Deputy Head, who glared at her with intense dislike.

This interview was tough. Six councillors who asked difficult questions about the curriculum and even school trips. After a long wait she was called in and offered the position as Headteacher.

She had to phone the Head in Tooting and ask if he could release her from the offer of Deputy Head. He could have said no, but he congratulated her and told her not to worry but accept the Headship. She wondered if he would have to advertise and interview all over again.

She phoned her mother. "I've got a Headship," she said exultantly.

"Oh," said her mother. "You would do better to get some qualification in cooking." No joy there.

She went back to Coventry thinking "I'm a Head. I'm a Head. I can't believe it." The job was not to start until the next September. It was now February.

That night she still said nothing to Jeremy. Robert had phoned her at Kenilworth, and she told him of her good news.

"I shall have to look for a house in Surrey," he said.

Ho! Ho! The Kenilworth house was now in her name, thanks to her mother. Already he was almost again assuming ownership.

"My father and I will look around," he had offered.

It seemed strange to say nothing to Jeremy. The final straw had probably been his suggestion that his parents move into his house. They would have had to have had the bedroom they slept in. She and Jeremy could not have slept in the box room. Impossible. But he hadn't talked about what the arrangements were or could be. Just like his decision to take William. It seemed to be his nature to make unilateral decisions.

Now *she* was making a unilateral decision. No way, come what may, was she going to turn a Headship down. This was her ultimate dream.

Very, very sadly she consulted an Estate Agent and put her house on the market. She knew that it would sell quickly because of the lovely gardens and general location. Kenilworth was a lovely village, and the approach to her house in a cul-de-sac, delightful.

She soon had several offers and the market price was reached. She agreed to the sale.

Robert said on the phone that he and his father were hunting for properties near to her future school and there were two strong possibilities. Both new, both detached. One in the grounds of an old vicarage but with a smallish plot, one in the grounds of an old manor house but with a large double plot. Robert sent her a sketch of the future house and it looked fine. The price was above the sale of the Kenilworth house. Her mother urged her not to get another mortgage. She said she would lend her the difference, but it was to be paid back monthly. Anne thanked her very much and the deposit was sent to the Estate Company for the house not yet built. The deed was done. For better or worse. Still, Anne had said nothing to Jeremy.

That weekend there was a get-together at his sister's house. All his family were there and they were invited. Anne wore a new dress that she had bought in a Kenilworth boutique. She would have said nothing, but suddenly one of the sisters started asking about Kenilworth. "Anne's house is lovely," she said. "Our Jeremy is so lucky. He would love living there."

Jeremy's mother joined in. "The garden is so big. A perfect place for children to play in."

Another sister joined in. "I don't know how they will get on with the sheepskin rugs. They seem to be all over the floor in the lounge."

Anne suddenly spoke up. "I have sold the house," she said.

"Sold it," gasped Jeremy's mother. Anne looked at Jeremy. He had gone ashen and did not speak.

"Oh well, you can buy another," one sister consoled.

Nothing else was said about the house until they got back to Jeremy's house.

"There are plenty of nice houses for sale," he offered. "I can find some from the Coventry Evening Telegraph."

Anne passed it off. The next night she still went to Jeremy's house. Jeremy produced a copy of the Evening Telegraph.

"There's a nice house for sale on the outskirts of Coventry. It's a nice detached house with a large garden."

He thrust the picture of the house into her hands. It wasn't as nice as Kenilworth in her opinion, but she could see that he was keen for her (or was it them) to have a detached house.

"I don't know why you have sold Kenilworth," queried Jeremy.

Anne hedged. "It isn't finally sold yet, "she stated. This was true. Completion hadn't yet taken place, but it was almost certain to be done.

The subject was dropped. The days proceeded as before. Anne told the Headmaster that she would be leaving for a Headship. He did not seem pleased with this and said, "I suppose it's a more modern school."

"No," said Anne. "I believe it is dated 1896 with a clock and bell tower." It had been unusual not to see the school before the interview. She thought it was rushed because it was assumed the present Deputy Head would get the position. She felt that she would have a problem with the Deputy Head who naturally had been very disappointed.

One Sunday, instead of going to her parents', Robert came and took Anne to see the school in Surrey. It was indeed quaint and quite historic. It also had a charm and was near to the Church, as it was a Church School. He then drove her to the plot where the house was being built seven miles from the School. It was a big plot, but in the front garden-to-be was a huge chestnut tree. "That has a preservation order on it," offered Robert. "Oh dear, too late now," thought Anne.

It all seemed strange. Robert did not drive her back but took her to the station at Euston where she caught the train. She caught the bus back to Kenilworth and then drove to Jeremy's house. A long day and she felt confused and exhausted.

Of course she was fond of Jeremy. She knew that in reality she thought more of him than he of her. If she had thought he loved her, she would never have considered going back to Robert. But there had been so many occasions, apart from the holiday, when he had been irritable if his boys were not with him, or when he wished Christine was still with him. She remembered how he had once actually whispered as she got into her car to go home, "I have never loved you, you know, it is just a way out." She had even tried to convince herself that she misheard him.

Robert was due to come the next Sunday. She made an excuse to Jeremy and went back to Kenilworth.

As she got in the house the telephone rang. "I'm sorry I can't come. I am having problems with my tyres. I will see you next week, ok." Robert rang off.

Problem with his tyres. Sounded very unlikely. A feeling of dread came over Anne. It didn't sound right. He didn't want to come. She had her new job, she had almost completed on the sale of her house. The new house was about to be built and he had problems with his tyres. There was a problem, and Anne was astute enough to know this. Had he got someone else and it was all starting again.

The next Sunday, when Robert had promised that he would come, the same thing happened. She had the house all ready, and again the phone rang. "I'm sorry I cannot come, my car is playing up."

Anne was getting frustrated. "What on earth is going on? I have just about sold the house. The solicitors have persuaded the clients not to move in until September. Luckily this does fall in with their plans. I am leaving my school all for you really. I was just getting settled. I am fond of Jeremy and I'm only 40 miles from my parents. I'm moving 140 miles away to an area I do not know and getting no support from you."

Robert offered a consolation. "I'm sorry, but it's not my fault. Look, in the half term break at Whitsun, I will book up a trip to Paris. I will book a package holiday at a good hotel. How about that?"

Anne was mollified. "That would be nice," she conceded.

"Well, I must sort this car out. I'll be in touch. Goodbye." Robert hung up.

Anne was really not happy. The bottom line was, that neither men seemed to want her for herself. She couldn't tell her parents of her concerns, because they had been sceptical anyway. It was clear that they were already concerned that she was making a huge mistake in going back to Robert.

Anne realised that she had rushed into things because of her uncertainties with Jeremy. Teaching full time and keeping the Kenilworth house going, she didn't have the chance to meet anyone new. She had met Mr Simpson through advertising, but she didn't want to do that again. Anyway, it was too late. Her beloved house was sold. The guilt at not originally moving with Robert had been the driving force. Had he got someone else now? Surely not. But the thought ate into her brain.

Jeremy seemed to have put the thought of Kenilworth on the back burner. Anne still enjoyed his love making and knew that she would miss this. Robert had made no moves in that direction at all. She didn't feel disloyal. She still felt single as she had seen Robert so little. When she visited Jeremy, she could see how close he was to Anthony and still felt an outsider. He told her that he was taking both boys camping at Whitsun. He was going to the Lake District. He seemed to assume that camping would not be for her, so she had no qualms about going to Paris with Robert.

Chapter 25

She had arranged to meet Robert at Luton airport and found no difficulty in parking the car. She met him at the check in. There was a courier and to her amazement the trip was labelled 'Honeymoon Trip'!

Upon arrival in Paris a coach took them to their hotel. Or was it? It seemed dark, dingy and airless. It appeared that only breakfast was provided. The bedroom too was dark and dingy with only a view of roofs. Not at all romantic and certainly not 'honeymoon'. She was very disappointed.

They had no vehicle. They had to walk to get meals, which seemed to be mainly in small dingy cafés. They took a coach trip (provided) to Versailles, but again Anne was disappointed in this. She had read about the Hall of Mirrors and expected splendour, chandeliers and magnificence. It seemed narrow and Anne couldn't imagine how the ladies used to swirl around in their enormous crinolines. The main problem, however, was Robert. Anne had bought some new clothes for the trip, but he didn't appear to notice or make any comment. He was quiet and polite, but seemed distant. At times he almost seemed like an automaton. He bought a postcard at Versailles and sat on a bench and scribbled on it. He had stamps. "I must just post this to someone," he said and as they were leaving found a post box.

Anne wondered to whom he was writing. Perhaps his mother, she thought hopefully, but again felt concern.

Robert did not attempt to make love to her, and Anne excused this to the fact that things were new and he felt embarrassed. But she was worried about his attitude. He seemed to become more and more remote. She decided that she disliked Paris. They didn't go into any shops, he didn't buy her anything and the time seemed to be spent hunting for cheap meals.

The hotel, or rather boarding house, was so depressing and Anne was not enjoying herself at all and apparently neither was Robert. Anne remembered the lovely holiday that she had had with Jeremy. In Naples their room had had single beds, but they had pushed these together and cuddled together all night.

The holiday was over and Anne felt relieved to be going back. Robert told her that the house in Godalming was only half built and would not be completed by September.

"The furniture at Kenilworth will have to go into storage," he informed her.

"I will arrange that with Pickfords, but I have to start school on the 4th September." Anne was worried. "Where do we stay? I thought there would be a direct move from Kenilworth to the house in Godalming. I assumed it would be completed."

"Well," said Robert, "you will be there to decide on things that can be changed. There are many things to decide, such as kitchen and bathroom tiles, flooring, the types of glass in bathrooms."

Anne had felt so detached from the house she hadn't considered all of this. "I suppose it would be better to be there," she conceded. "But where will we stay?"

"Don't worry," said Robert. "I will arrange somewhere temporarily."

Anne still felt confused with the situation. She loved Kenilworth and didn't really have her heart in organising another house. She had been content with the one she had.

Robert said more to her at the end of the holiday and on the coach and at the airport than he had done from the whole trip. Back at Luton, Robert again said that he would be in touch, and he drove back to London and she to Kenilworth.

She looked at her house after she drove back. She had chosen the bathroom tiles then – or rather they had together. Her mother had paid the extra for the parquet floor downstairs and the orchid and autumn leaf glass in the front door and bathroom. She would also have to start again with lawns and flower beds. She tried not to think about it.

The holiday had certainly not been a success. Who had he been writing to? He seemed almost desperate to post the card. She had had no contact with Jeremy but knew that he was away from Saturday to Saturday as was she. He would be home tomorrow on Sunday.

Anne mowed the lawns yet again and spent some time looking at the television. She drove to Jeremy's on Sunday night. He seemed very pleased to see her and said that they had found a good campsite. He looked well and happy. He had obviously enjoyed being with his sons. He seemed to assume that she had been to Wellingborough with her parents. She just said nothing and he probably thought that perhaps she wished that she had been with them after all.

In fact, she did wish that she had been with them. She felt that she hated Paris and never wanted to go there again. Everyone said how wonderful it was, The Louvre, The Notre Dame, but all she seemed to have done was go up and down the metro stairs looking for cheap places to eat as Robert said food was so expensive in good hotels. She hadn't really seen Paris at all. They had walked beside the Seine, but Robert had seemed so glum.

Jeremy enthused about the Lake District and said that she would have loved the scenery. "I would love to live there," he said.

Chapter 26

As time rolled on, Anne met the family buying her house. Before, the estate agents had shown them round when she was at school. A very nice family with two children. Anne had to say that she would be taking the curtains and light fittings, but would leave the small garden shed. Robert was arranging to have the boat taken to his parents' garage. It brought it home to Anne that this part of her life was nearly over.

The children in her school knew that she was leaving and presented her with a coffee table. Not her style of course but she was grateful for the thought. There seemed to be no news of a new Deputy Head appointment. Anne wondered if Mr Roberts would at last have the Deputy Head from the staff that he had wanted.

Jeremy didn't seem to grasp that she was moving south. Her father said that he would help Robert sort things out for the move.

Anne felt a strong tie to Jeremy. He had helped her over a bad patch and although he had been moody and difficult on occasions, he had still been there in the end, and there when people seemed to shun her. She thought Jeremy still thought that they would end up together. She had told him about the house being built at Godalming and he accepted that she was moving for a Headship. He seemed to think that Robert was superfluous. He had left her, it was broken and could not be repaired. He had realised that she was ambitious. He even stated that there was a branch of his firm at Dunsfold a few miles from her new house and intimated that he could get a transfer. Strangely enough, Jeremy seemed more at peace now. Perhaps he too thought a new life for him beckoned.

The day came for her to leave. She put the most precious things she had in her car and packed clothes. Robert had telephoned an address for her to go to in Guildford, seven miles from her school. She had to stop and ask the way several times, but eventually she found it.

A large old Victorian house divided into bedsits. It was dark and gloomy. The landlady was there and showed her to a large room. There was a white inset cupboard for clothes, a double bed, a table and chairs, and that was about it.

"Where do we cook?" enquired Anne.

"Oh, there is the use of the kitchen next door."

"Where is the bathroom?"

"Oh, that's along the corridor."

Robert was not coming this day. He and her father were organising the clearing of Kenilworth to go into storage.

She emptied the car and put her clothes in the white cupboard. The bed was made up. She sat down and wondered how long she would have to live like this.

She had a few provisions with her, so made tea from the large kitchen next door, and ate some sausage rolls.

She knew that she could find the school tomorrow and fell asleep.

CHAPTER 27

A nne introduced herself to the staff and took assembly. There were no Registers made up, so Anne and the Secretary had to do these quickly from typed lists. The previous Headmaster had apparently locked himself in his office writing a book. There were timetables, however. It was a small school of 180 children and six teaching staff. Lunch was served in a prefabricated building on the edge of the playground and meals were brought in. There were two dinner ladies, Mrs Hicks and Mrs Scott, and the caretaker, Mr Elliot. The Chair of Governors was the Vicar Rev. Bowman.

The children were delightful and very well behaved. Several parents called in to see her and later the Infant Headteacher called in to welcome her.

Robert did not appear that night nor the next day. Anne phoned her parents from the school phone. Her mother answered and said that Kenilworth had been cleared. Everything had gone to storage. Robert had brought her father home and shaken Elizabeth's hand. He had said that he was sorry for all that had occurred, but everything would now be alright. He had presumably gone back to his parents' house.

After the next day at school, Robert came to the bedsit. Anne didn't quite know how to describe it, but their main living quarters was just the one big room. Anne felt that Robert could have found better accommodation.

When they got married (Robert only three months out of university), they had been almost penniless, but the flat he had found was spacious. Very nicely fully furnished with two bedrooms. This accommodation, however, was minimalist, and the room seemed grubby and downmarket. Could Robert not have found something better? There seemed to be no facility for washing as there was no washing machine in the kitchen. Anne had noticed a launderette near to her school so she would have to use that she supposed.

Robert told her that the house at Kenilworth was completely cleared and that her father had worked very hard. He also said that the removal men were very helpful. Anne had to put that house out of her mind, but it seemed strange to think that everything was somewhere in a storage unit. Robert had bought some groceries, sausage and chips, which they managed to cook in the kitchen adjacent to their room.

Anne told Robert about the school and said that she thought she would be happy there.

The next day Robert caught a train to London and Anne drove to school.

Halfway through the morning the phone rang in her office. It had been put through by the Secretary.

"Is that the Godalming Primary School?"

"It is," replied Anne. "Who's speaking please?"

"It is Jessica."

"I'm sorry, who is Jessica. Do I know you?"

"I don't know. I am Robert's girlfriend. I don't know why you are bothering him. He has told me that you followed him from Kenilworth. He has admitted that he is still married, but he told me at first that he was divorced. I thought I was going to marry him. When he told me you were on your way down, I hit him in the face and his spectacles went under a bus. I then went to a pub and got drunk. I have just had a baby, but it's not Robert's. I wanted to keep it, but he made me get it adopted. He has put me in a dingy flat in Paddington."

What could Anne say? It didn't make sense. Robert was with Marilyn in January. It was now September. Jessica must have been quite pregnant when Robert went out with her – or was it really Robert's baby? Robert had always seemed so fastidious. She couldn't imagine him going out with a pregnant girl. This was her worst nightmare.

Anne just said, "I'm sorry, but I am at school. I cannot discuss this. You must sort this out with Robert."

"Is it true that you are having a house built in Godalming?" asked the girl.

"It is, but unfortunately it won't be ready for a few months."

"Did you buy it?"

"I did."

"My father took me to see your house at Kenilworth. I liked the rose beds outside. I half expected to see you on the doorstep. Do you know that Robert came to see me in hospital nearly every day after work when I had the baby. I told him that I wanted to keep it and he said, "I knew you'd say that."

Horror of horrors. Anne felt sick. How terrible if he had forced her to have the child adopted even if it wasn't his. Surely the girl's family could have helped her. If her father was so interested to see where Robert had lived, perhaps they would have cared for the child. Anne knew that Robert would not dare tell his parents about a baby. All the time that he had been cajoling Anne to sell Kenilworth he had been going out with Jessica. He had told her that Marilyn left him for another man after a dance. Perhaps Marilyn left him because he had started going out with Jessica. What was the truth? There was just a web of lies. She had been right to be suspicious, when he had said his car had broken down or the tyres and wheels were troublesome when he hadn't come to see her.

"I'm very sorry," continued Anne, "but I must get on with my job. It really isn't fair for you to ring me at work. Goodbye."

She put down the phone and hoped the Secretary, Mrs Wright, in the next office hadn't been listening in.

It had all been bad enough before, but this certainly didn't seem like the Robert she had married. She really would have liked children herself, despite her career. In the early days she had mentioned having a baby to Robert and his answer had been, "I'm not bothered." Now she just could not imagine him walking round London with a pregnant girl, leading them both along with a string of lies and false promises, and even worse, insisting that Jessica's baby be adopted. Whether or not it was his, there was no excuse for his selfish and cruel behaviour.

Anne had a job to do that day. Luckily events at school pushed the mind-blowing conversation out of her mind temporarily.

CHAPTER 28

After school she phoned Jeremy. He was stilted and clearly annoyed that she was down south. The staff had gone home and of course the children. She was crying by the phone, what could she do? What should she do? She thought. The caretaker, Mr Elliot came in and saw her crying. He was a dear soul and must have thought something at school had upset her.

"I expect it's been a long day," he said kindly.

"I am used to long days," replied Anne tactfully. "Have you been at this school for a long time."

"A very long time," said Mr Elliot.

"Do you live close by."

"In a bungalow, in the next road to the school. I will tell you a story. I married a woman who had a daughter and bungalow. I was in love at the time. But now all the love has died. All she thought about was her daughter and still does. We won a duvet at Bingo. Straight away she took it to her daughter."

Anne didn't quite know how to answer this. "They do say true love never dies. Think of Shakespeare. 'Love is not love which alters when it altercation finds, nor bends with the remover to remove.'"

"Well, mine has died," responded Mr Elliot. "I don't know why I'm telling you all this, but I've had a bad day today with the wife. You look an understanding woman."

"Thank you," replied Anne – thinking that his day could not have been worse than hers.

She bade him goodnight and drove home. She felt weary and almost lightheaded. Her eyes drooped. Suddenly she realised that she had almost dropped to sleep and thump! Her car hit the brickwork of a central crossing where a bollard was situated. She was lucky she did not hit it head on. Sighing, she called the AA. Very quickly they appeared. Her tyre was shredded. "We can fit your spare," they offered. "You must be annoyed at this."

"Thank you so much," retorted Anne. "I am only grateful that I was not killed, however."

Robert was in the bedsit when she got back. "You are late," he retorted. "I brought fish and chips home and they will be cold."

"I don't really feel hungry," replied Anne. "I had to contact the AA as I shredded a tyre. However, I received a phone call from Jessica."

Robert went pale. "What had she to say?"

Anne relayed to him all that had transpired.

Robert blustered, "I did think of marrying her once," he confessed. "But she is untidy and messy. I couldn't live with her."

"But how could you let the baby be adopted?"

"It wasn't mine. She always said that she would have it adopted. I had to help her in the beginning because her family didn't want to help."

"If Jessica's father had driven her to see the house at Kenilworth, that seemed pretty caring and concerned for her possible future," Anne thought.

"It seems as if you found her a flat," continued Anne.

"She has to live somewhere. She pays for it. It was just a rebound thing after Marilyn."

Anne was too weary to continue the discussion. What should she do? She was now down south and the Headteacher of a school. Could she really now go through a divorce? The first documents on the divorce had probably been cancelled. They were out of date now anyway. As a Headteacher she felt that perhaps a divorce was not now a great idea.

Perhaps Jessica was exaggerating. Perhaps it wasn't his baby and he had been lonely in London. She didn't really convince herself, but felt that she missed Jeremy. She felt that she could never really trust Robert again. He always appeared plausible, but her instinct told her that Jessica had been speaking the truth. She had to go through with the house at Godalming as well. The deposit was paid and it was projected to be completed in March. All her furniture and main belongings were in storage. She had made a decision. Let Robert see his Jessica and talk things through. At the weekend she would go to Coventry and see Jeremy. Robert had left her for Marilyn, now there was a Jessica. If she had known all this, of course, she would not have left Kenilworth. Robert had at first appeared so genuine that it was really the train journey to London that disorientated him. She had also felt so guilty that she had not encouraged him to take up the offer of alternative employment at Hatfield where the new offices would be.

But, she had not bargained for Jessica.

"Go to Jessica and try to sort things out. Sadly it seems as if she really loves you and really wanted to marry you. I shall go back to Coventry on Saturday."

CHAPTER 29

Anne phoned Jeremy after school the next day and told him she was coming to Coventry. At first he demurred, but then said he would be there for her.

On Saturday, Anne left her car at the station and took the train to London. She had to go to Euston and then caught the bus to Jeremy's house from Coventry station. Anne didn't quite know what to tell Jeremy. He had half thought she had gone down south only for the Headship and just took it for granted that she would have another detached house. He quite accepted that it was on a double plot and was a new build.

She told him mainly about the school and the staff. She did say that Robert had a new girlfriend called Jessica. Jeremy was not surprised at this at all.

Anthony went to a neighbour's house. Anne and Jeremy once again went to the cinema. Jeremy made love to her and Anne thought ruefully that it was no wonder Robert had shown no interest in her at all if he had Jessica.

Jeremy prepared a salad for lunch and they all went for a drive into the Warwickshire countryside.

Anne had to get back to Guildford, of course, for school the next day. Jeremy drove her to the station quoting "Sunday bloody Sunday".

Anne agreed to come back the next week and Jeremy seemed contented with this. Anne felt that Robert's betrayal was one too many and felt that she was always 'the bad guy'.

Jessica had seemed so indignant that she had come down south and Anne felt that they were probably both victims.

The next week carried on as before. Robert came to the bedsit in the evenings and didn't mention Jessica.

The landlady who owned the building in which the bedsit was situated was probably in her late thirties. She had a young son. She had looked in, the previous week, and asked if everything was alright. To Anne's surprise, however, later in the week Anne was in the room in the evening and Robert was not yet back.

The landlady opened the door without knocking and said sharply, "Isn't Robert home yet?"

Anne was startled. It was obvious that Robert wasn't there, but why was the landlady concerned? Perhaps he hadn't paid the rent. Anne had no idea how much it was, but had left it to Robert to organise this time.

"I'm afraid not," said Anne. "May I help you?"

"Oh no, I just wondered if he was in." She left.

Robert soon came in.

"The landlady seemed to want you," stated Anne. "Is there a problem?"

"I pay the rent monthly until we leave. I haven't a clue what she wanted," answered Robert.

Anne's instincts were once again aroused. She didn't even know the landlady's name but the look on her face when she burst in worried her. The woman seemed most disturbed that Robert was not in. Did she worry so about all her tenants?

The next evening Anne noticed that the landlady had caught Robert as he came in the door. They were talking together and seemed very friendly.

When Robert came in Anne queried this.

"Oh we travel up to London on the same train in the morning. She has inherited several properties from her family and some are in London. There are a lot rented and she has an office in London and staff. She is a very clever woman."

"Why does she live here in Guildford?"

"Her son is at school here; he has a nanny. There are also more of her family here."

Anne had a feeling that Robert was interested in this woman and she with him. She was tall and thin, with mousey brown permed hair. She appeared a lot older than Robert and Anne couldn't imagine any attraction from her to him. But she was suspicious. Surely not another one, thought Anne. Surely not. Anne was giving up on Robert completely.

She went back to Coventry, this time after school on Friday night. There was nothing to go back for to the bedsit. Jeremy had some news for her.

"That girl Jessica phoned me," he offered.

"How on earth could she have found out your telephone number? It can only have been from Robert. I gave it to him ages ago in case of an emergency."

"Well, she phoned. She asked if I could handle you and I said, No problem."

Anne thought Robert must have made her out to be a termagant. She didn't like the fact that Jessica had managed to get Jeremy's number from Robert. She was probably delighted that Anne had returned to Jeremy and was sounding out the ground to see if this could be the opportunity for her to have Robert to herself. Probably still hoping for marriage.

Jeremy seemed amused by it, but then the next day came a postcard. It had no message. His address was clearly printed, but the picture was of a duck carrying a swag of money with the words, 'Money bags'. Jeremy still seemed unscathed by this, but Anne felt harassed. The phone call to her school, then to Jeremy, now this. What more was the girl capable of? It was beginning to feel like a horror movie.

They had a nice weekend and Anne of course returned to Guildford.

Robert was unfazed by her information about Jessica.

"I did not give her the phone number or address," he indignantly stated.

"It is the only way she could have found out," retorted Anne.

"Well, there is the telephone directory," replied Robert.

"That is ridiculous," responded Anne. "I don't believe you. You must have given her the number."

Robert made no reply.

"Where did you go this weekend?" asked Anne. No answer.

"What did you do?" insisted Anne.

"We went camping near to Chichester," admitted Robert. "I had a tent at my parents and gas bottles etc, from my time with Marilyn."

Anne had been to Jeremy's so she could say nothing.

Chapter 30

The only amusing thing was that they were invited by the Vicar for dinner on the Thursday. Anne put on a lovely dress and over her shoulders a musquash stole with tails that she had had for a long time. She put it over the back of her chair during the dinner and the Vicar's dog ate all the tails off the stole. The Vicar and his wife were mortified, but Anne couldn't stop laughing. He had done it so neatly, it actually looked better without them.

Poor Barney, the dog, was told to stand in the corner like a child, but Anne gave him a stroke and told him that he was a good dog.

The same pattern continued. Anne going to Jeremy at the weekend and Robert going out with Jessica. Anne did visit the house after school and it was nearly built. She met the developers and organised some improvements inside, such as an extended kitchen, removing the utility room. Once again she ordered parquet flooring, fully tiled bathrooms (there were two), and arches with wrought iron gates each side of the house, as at Kenilworth. She also arranged for the garden to be turfed. The house was of Georgian design with small square window panes. Anne asked for bull's eye windows to be interspersed in the front bow window.

Choosing bathroom fittings, tiles and patterns of glass for bathroom windows, etc, took her mind away from Robert. At the end of the day, she was buying the house with the money from the sale of Kenilworth. It was her house and she decided that she would make it as similar to Kenilworth as possible. She arranged for two ponds to be put in place and chose fir trees to edge the rear of the large garden.

Anne still continued to see Jeremy at the weekend, because, as of yet, she could do nothing in the house. Robert was obviously still seeing Jessica but stayed at the bedsit in the week. They were now more like a brother and sister although totally dissimilar in personality. They talked of day-to-day matters. Anne talked about the house. They even chose some of the tiles together from samples Anne had gathered from the builders.

At last, the house was ready.

Robert had hired Pickfords when clearing Kenilworth, so the same firm were now delivering the contents of storage to the house. It was the Easter holidays. Jeremy was taking his boys camping again.

The removal men turned up at four o'clock. They said that this was their second job of the day. They appeared tired and dispirited. Anne wanted the furniture in the same positions roughly where possible as at Kenilworth. The men moved quickly. They were obviously keen to get home.

Robert had already arranged for the light fittings to be in situ. The house began to look more like a home. The curtains from Kenilworth fitted the windows, and Robert put these up. Rails were in place. The builders had agreed to fit venetian blinds to the kitchen windows and only the dressing room had no curtains.

Anne had corresponded with her mother's solicitor in Wellingborough and they had handled all financial transactions. The builders were going to organise the garden with a contractor to lay all the garden turf. The patio was down, red drive in place, ponds in place, wrought iron gates at the side of the house sorted.

They had left the bedsit for good earlier that day. They had little there and Anne was glad to leave.

They gave the removal men a tip before they left. They had worked well and been obliging, even though they were tired.

Anne managed to find some bed linen and after making some tea she had brought with her and with only a few biscuits to eat, they fell into bed at about midnight, exhausted.

The gardeners came to lay the turf the next day and Anne drove to a corner shop for some groceries. Robert said he had to go back to the bedsit.

"I thought we brought everything," queried Anne.

"I haven't settled the account," countered Robert.

"But you paid monthly from your bank," stated Anne.

"I must just check that it is all settled," said Robert. He drove off. Anne thought this strange, but she had plenty to do putting things in order. The cutlery had to be sorted, plates and dishes put into the kitchen cupboards. The ornaments were still in boxes. There were mirrors to be hung. She was busy all day.

The telephone people came and installed the phone, and an aerial company fitted the television aerial. Anne had bought a lovely television in a walnut case when at Kenilworth, and she was happy to see it again. She had given her old television to Jeremy.

The lawn was laid. The builders had left a broom and Anne swept the patio.

Robert was still not home. Had he gone to see Jessica? "He really should be here to help, there was so much to do," she thought.

The day progressed and finally Robert returned.

"The landlady wasn't in," he explained. "I had to wait for her to come in. Anyway, everything's sorted."

He did help Anne unpack boxes that were in the garage and then fetched fish and chips from a local shop, so they had some food.

Robert finished hanging curtains and Anne made up the other beds. There were four bedrooms, one ensuite. This was a plus as Kenilworth only had one bathroom.

The next day Robert said he had to go into work.

"I thought you were having time off for the Easter holiday?" queried Anne.

"Oh, it isn't that simple. We don't get school holidays you know."

Off he drove. There was still so much to do. She phoned her parents and told them that the house was nearly organised.

CHAPTER 31

S he was hanging some antique plates on the walls of the
sitting room, when the phone rang.

"Hello," she said, thinking "Who on earth knows this
number already?".

"It's Jessica."

"Oh no!" thought Anne.

Jessica continued, "I think Robert's having an affair with
the landlady at the bedsit in Guildford. I came there you
know, when you were away. I guess you didn't know that,
and I slept in your bed. I saw the landlady kiss Robert in the
kitchen. I also found some condoms in his pocket and I don't
need these as I'm on the pill. Robert is nearly giving me a
nervous breakdown. He almost promised to marry me, I am
very upset."

Anne didn't know what to say. She was not really
surprised to hear about the landlady and believed Jessica.
If he was sleeping with Jessica, why would he start an affair
with the landlady? The woman was plain and uninteresting
and seemed older than Robert.

"If I asked Robert, I think he would leave you again. Why
can't you let him go? He obviously doesn't want you."

Anne replied, "After Marilyn, Robert asked me to forgive
him and start again. It was he that persuaded me to sell the
house and move down south. I was fortunate in gaining
a Headship and that was the factor in the house being at
Godalming. It is quite close to my school."

"Well I'd like to see you and talk to you. I'll send you my address and you can talk to me face to face," said Jessica.

"I'm sorry," said Anne. "I have so much to do. I must get on, goodbye." Anne put the phone down.

It seemed that Robert was completely out of control. Never in a million years had she imagined he could behave as he was doing. She reflected once again, how quiet and studious he had been at Leicester when they met and when they became engaged, polite and courteous. He seemed like a Jekyll and Hyde character now.

The fact that Jessica had phoned indicated that Robert was not with her today. He was probably with the landlady at Guildford she mused, and not at work as he said. That too had seemed unlikely.

She phoned her parents again and told them of the phone call.

"Do not go to see this girl," her mother warned. "Your father could not believe that you were going back to Robert as you know. But what a hypocrite. He shook my hand and said how sorry he was about all that had happened and how he would make it up to you."

"I can't get into all the divorce business again," replied Anne. "I have the Headship and must concentrate on that. The house here is quite nice. I shall never love it as I loved Kenilworth. The area around here still seems strange, but I suppose I shall get used to it."

"Your father is too upset to speak to you," said her mother. "I think that he would like to throttle Robert. But you know that we are always here for you."

Anne thanked her mother and put the phone down. No, she wouldn't go to see Jessica. What good would it do? Robert had admitted that she was 14 years younger than him, so that made her 22. Just a bit older than Anne when she married. She had been 21 in the December, but 22 on 13th January. This girl seemed immature for her age. Almost child-like.

Robert came home at eight o'clock. By then Anne had managed to hang most of the antique plates and mirrors. The only real problem was the Kemble Minx piano that her mother had bought her for their first house in Coventry. It didn't fit into the sitting room. It had to be put into an alcove in the dining room. This was a pity, because it was not so accessible to play.

The days went by. Robert went out each day at 8am and came home at 8pm. Anne continued to put final touches to the house. She drove to a nearby nursery and bought plants.

One evening Robert did not come home. No phone call. She knew that there had been no accident and guessed he was with Jessica. "Why had he not let the divorce go ahead," she thought. "Why hadn't he made good on his promise to marry Jessica?"

She pondered this and came up with an answer. Robert's father had not been pleased that Robert had given up his share of the Kenilworth house. Robert had confessed this to her. She guessed he had told his parents nothing about Jessica.

Robert's father had wanted him to be settled again in a house and here it was. Robert had always been rather afraid of his father and desperate for his good opinion. Here was the answer. All this subterfuge for a house. Robert's father thought his son once more nicely settled in a detached house. She knew that Robert's father had indeed helped him to hunt for a house near to her school. How little his parents really knew. Did they even know that it was she that had bought it outright?

CHAPTER 32

Anne phoned Jeremy. He had again had a good time camping with the boys and was now home. Anne just told him that the house was almost organised and he said that he would like to see it. Robert came back that night and did not deny his affair with the landlady.

"She seemed desperate," he offered as an excuse. "It was only a few times and it didn't really work out. I'm not seeing her again."

Anne didn't know whether or not to believe him. Still what did it matter? It had happened yet again and Robert had changed out of all recognition.

"I have to go to a conference this weekend," he stated. "I shall be back on Monday night."

Anne was almost past caring. She did recount to him all of the conversation with Jessica, but he was disinterested. He did say, "Well I don't know how she got this number so quickly," but Anne was getting used to lie after lie.

The next day she phoned Jeremy and asked him down to see the house. He said that Anthony would go to his mother to be with William, and he would drive down. Anne gave him the directions.

On Saturday Jeremy arrived. He was delighted with the house and thought it wonderful that there were two bathrooms. He wasn't surprised that Robert wasn't there, as he knew about Jessica. Anne drove Jeremy around the area. Surrey has some lovely scenery and Jeremy was very happy.

On the Sunday, Anne drove Jeremy to Wittering, which was the nearest seaside. They had a meal at a lovely old fashioned inn and Anne drove Jeremy back to the house. He was in a very good mood and at his most charming. He told her that he would always be her 'anchor' and would always be there for her. If he had been like this all the time at Kenilworth, Anne would never have left. She desperately needed to feel wanted. Being with Robert now was like being buffeted hither and thither.

They parted sadly, and Jeremy had to drive back to Coventry. A long way.

Robert developed a pattern of not appearing at the house. He said he was staying with a male colleague and as payment giving him a bottle of whisky. Anne knew this to be a lie.

She returned to school and was happy there. The Deputy Head was a bit awkward, but the children were delightful. The days passed quickly. She had to order stock and equipment for the school. She managed to form a choir and they put on a concert for the parents. Robert seldom came home in the evening.

Anne began to return to Coventry regularly at the weekends. She mowed the lawns at the house on Friday evening, and dusted and then went to Coventry by train on the Saturday. Sometimes Jeremy was playing cricket, so she passed the time at the hairdressers. He would often pick her up afterwards. Anthony was with a neighbour.

A hotel in Kenilworth held a dance on Saturday evenings. Sometimes they went to that. Jeremy hadn't been able to dance, but he was very versatile and soon picked it up and they had some pleasant evenings.

He provided the lunch on Sundays and sometimes they went to her parents. As said before, Elizabeth liked Jeremy, and Howard enjoyed talking about fishing and shooting. They couldn't stay long because Anne had to catch the train back to London and then to Guildford station. She often had a taxi home but sometimes there was a bus.

She never knew if Robert would be at home. Sometimes he was. It became custom and practice for him not to appear in the week, but he seemed to be there on Sunday.

Anne always seemed to be mowing the lawn on Friday evening and decided to obtain a gardener. There was an advertisement in the local paper offering gardening services and Anne responded. The next week she met Mr Owen, who said that his father had been the main gardener for Cranleigh Public School. He was happy to use her mower which was an electric Atco. They settled on a rate of £12 an hour and he offered to mow the lawns on Friday morning. Anne gave him the key to the double garage and said she would leave his money inside the mower box. Another problem solved.

Anne had her salary paid monthly but Robert offered nothing towards expenses. He obviously thought that the house was hers and therefore it was her responsibility to pay all the expenses. Anne did find it difficult. She still had her car which she drove to school, but there was the road tax and petrol to pay. She also had to pay for the telephone, electric, gas and community charge when it was due. She was also putting money by for a new car. Money was tight. She did not ask Robert for money, because he appeared so seldom. He still seemed to think, however, that he could come and go as he pleased.

CHAPTER 33

O ne day, Anne had a shock. By chance she came home from school early. She had invited the secretary from school to visit that evening and she wished to prepare.

As she opened the front door she was met with a wave of black smoke. In a panic, she rushed upstairs, thinking she had left the electric blanket on. There was black smoke everywhere, but the plug for the blanket was off. She rushed down to the kitchen, thinking it must be coming from the gas boiler, but no.

She went into the sitting room. To her horror the settee was burning. It had caught fire to the carpet and the velvet curtains. Without thinking she tried to drag the settee out of the house. Immediately it burst into yellow flames. She was lucky her clothing didn't catch fire. She left it burning on the drive and rushed back inside. The phone was intact. She phoned Robert at work in desperation and phoned the fire brigade. She managed to put out the smouldering curtains and stamp out the burning carpet. Everywhere was covered in a black tar-like substance. The settee had somehow caught fire but had just slowly smouldered. The carpet was ruined. She couldn't see all the damage, and the smell was deadly.

The fire brigade came but the fires in the sitting room were out. They said they thought it was an electrical fault, but how was not apparent. The settee had burned itself on the drive.

Robert arrived. Anne had of course already phoned the school secretary and told her of the situation.

It was impossible to stay in the house. Anne was insured with the Royal Insurance Company and said she would have to contact them the next day from school.

Robert suggested he drove her to his parents in Carshalton. Anne was covered in black soot. She managed to find something in the wardrobe upstairs, a suit and jacket. They locked the house and went to Carshalton. Robert's mother was not pleased to see them. She offered no bath or shower to Anne who was grubby. She reluctantly provided a meal, and complained that Anne had taken too much meat from the dish provided. This was not true of course. Afterwards, as it was late, Anne and Robert went to the bedroom they shared there many years ago. They got up early and Robert drove Anne back to the house to pick up her car which was parked outside the house, luckily not on the drive. Anne had managed to clean herself up. Robert drove off and Anne went to school. She obviously told the staff what had happened and the news filtered through to the Infant Head Teacher.

Anne told the Infant Headteacher, Miss Truss, what a dreadful reception she had had from Robert's parents and that it was impossible for her to live in her own house.

"Would you like to stay with me?" she offered. She named a price and Anne accepted gratefully.

Anne phoned the Royal Insurance Company and their response was superb. They offered to meet her after school to pick up the keys to the house and said that they would remove all the damaged items, dry clean and clean all that was necessary and remove all traces of smoke damage.

Robert appeared at the house. Anne told him that she could not stay with his parents as she was not welcome, but would be staying with the Infant Headteacher.

Robert seemed very happy with this arrangement. He could have offered an alternative arrangement for them both to go to a hotel, but he didn't. He also just seemed to assume that Anne would sort it all out with her Insurance Company. He offered no help whatsoever.

Anne found some more clothes untouched by smoke and tar and drove to the home of Miss Truss. The Infant Headteacher was wonderful.

It was predicted that the repairs to the house would take six months, but Robert made no contact with her at all. He did not enquire about progress or how she was managing.

Anne went to Jeremy at the weekend and in the week had to have time from school to go to London to order a new suite, a new carpet and new lampshades. After school she resprayed gold edged mirrors. She cleaned the tarnished silver and washed the ornaments. Every night after school she spent time at the house before returning to the Infant Headteacher, Miss Truss.

She arranged for a local builder to redecorate the house and a carpenter to replace the damaged wood in the bow window and parquet floor. Even the outside of the house had to be redecorated. The top half of the Georgian house was white, and smoke had even infiltrated out of the windows onto this.

It was a mammoth task, but she was so grateful to the Insurance Company. They cleaned everything and even the tiles in the kitchen and bathrooms were covered in a black residue. Unfortunately, the Insurance cover was not new for old, and she had to honestly list the present day cost of the items at second-hand value. Anne had a struggle with money. Her mother offered to replace all the curtains. She had provided them at Kenilworth and had the same measurements and had them professionally made. She had them sent to the house, boxed by courier.

Anne had insufficient money to pay the workers and had to explain that there was a delay. She had had to pay for the suite and carpet from her own money, plus other items. It was all a nightmare.

She was so grateful to the Infant Headteacher and had tried not to be a nuisance by going to a launderette for her washing and to a sauna in Godalming for a shower.

CHAPTER 34

Jeremy had been very kind when she went to Coventry at the weekend. The Infant Head probably thought she was either going to Robert or her parents, but she didn't ask. She just knew that Anne left on Friday and returned on Sunday evening. Most of the time Anne drove to Coventry. She went via Oxford and Banbury.

At the end of six months, the house was back to its former glory. The new suite and carpet had been delivered. One of the male parents at her school, hearing of her plight, had kindly put the carpet down. It was a very, very large patterned Wilton rug, which covered the whole floor. The dining carpet had been cleaned. All the tiles were sparkling clean. The windows had been cleaned. All wood repaired and painted.

There was a bit of a hiccup because the money for the carpentry and decoration had not come through from the Insurance Company. She received a threatening letter, but luckily the money did arrive at last.

Robert eventually phoned her at school. "How is it going?" he asked. It was the first time he had spoken to her in six months. She guessed he had told his parents that he was with her, whilst spending time with Jessica.

"It's just about back to normal," Anne said.

"Oh well, I'll come this evening." That evening he strode in as if nothing had happened.

Anne felt very bitter. She had spent hours after school respraying mirror surrounds with gold paint. She had had to search Godalming to find suitable lampshades for those that could not be cleaned. She had been short of money and sold a valuable necklace from her Godmother, Lady Rundle, to raise cash to replace irreversibly damaged items. The Insurance Company had been excellent, but she had had to itemise everything and deal with any problems. She had had to find the decorators and carpenters. She had had to organise all the cleaning and washing of bed linen, covers and clothing.

Now here he was strutting his stuff as if he hadn't a care in the world. If the situation was reversed Anne would have helped him.

Anne felt that it was cruel the way he was behaving. He seemed to have no thought for anyone than himself. She didn't think he had any intention of ever marrying Jessica who still seemed to be hanging on hopefully.

Two parcels had arrived at the house. They were addressed to her. She opened them. There were two books inside entitled 'The Failed Marriage' and 'How to Divorce your Husband'. There was a note inside.

Here is my address. When you come I will grease the step. Be there on Tuesday at 7 o'clock.

Jessica.

That was today, the post must have been delayed.

The phone rang. Robert answered the phone. Anne could only guess the question.

"No, she's not coming."

Robert had gone pale. It was clear that Jessica was not pleased.

Robert did stay that evening, but little was spoken.

The next evening was a Governing Body Meeting at the school. The Governors met in her office and the School Secretary stayed to provide tea, coffee and biscuits.

The Vicar spoke when everyone was seated. "The D.E.S. have finally granted permission for a new First School to be built at Binscombe. This school will close at the end of next year and may become a Community Centre. There will be no admissions that year from The Infant School. The top year will be leaving. The other years will be housed in mobile units at The Infant School."

The Vicar turned to Anne. "I am sure you are wondering where this leaves you. Well, we all think you have done a wonderful job here and we will recommend you for Headship of the Binscombe First School."

Anne was stunned. When will the school be built, she thought. Everyone seemed to be talking and the meeting broke up quickly.

The Vicar spoke to her. "We had applied for this to happen a long time ago, but had no response. That is why we appointed a new Head here. This is a very old building and quite outdated. I am sure that you will be appointed to the new school when it is built. Please don't worry."

Anne replied, "I am old and ugly enough to look after myself." She felt betrayed and bitter and drove home. She was wise enough to realise that a new school would take some time to build and there would have to be fresh interviews for the Headship of a new school.

Robert did not appear that night, but when the Times Educational Supplement came out, Anne bought one. She searched the advertisements. She found an advertisement for a Headship in Richmond. She applied immediately. Within days she received a reply and was called for an interview. It was another Church School.

She drove to the school taking time out from her school. It was quite a journey as it was before the M25 opened. She had to drive to Esher, and into Richmond. She had time to view the school before the interview.

The interviews were in the school library with eight Governors present, once again including the Vicar. Again she was offered the position, to commence at the beginning of the next term. She accepted the position but on the way home was unsure. Could she really do this journey every day? There was a lot of traffic on the road and she began to feel doubtful.

Robert was at the house which had been named Beaumont, the same name of the house as Kenilworth. Robert never had produced the new nameplate he promised, but Jeremy, being a carpenter and quite gifted, had made her a lovely one, black letters on golden wood at Kenilworth and this had been in the store.

She had told Robert that the Godalming School was closing and now informed him that she had obtained another Headship. She expressed her concerns about the distance and the busy roads. Robert suggested that she could travel by train from Guildford to Waterloo and then catch a train to St Margarets, close to her school. Much relieved at this suggestion, the next day she informed The Governing Body of the Godalming School that she was leaving at the end of the term.

Robert surprised her. He said that he would drive her to Guildford station and travel with her to Waterloo, until she got used to the journey. He also promised to meet her at Waterloo, when possible, for the journey home.

The term continued until it was time to leave. There was a Leaving Assembly and she was presented with a Parker Pen set, by the Deputy, who was now, to that lady's joy, to be the Acting Head.

CHAPTER 35

The first day at the new school was pleasant. A very nice welcoming staff, a male supportive Deputy Head and an excellent Secretary in situ. Anne had a lovely big office and there was the dearest caretaker, Mr Simms. He was so obliging and even offered to take any laundry to a cleaning company in St Margarets.

She once again formed a choir and they sang in the nearby church on a couple of occasions.

Unfortunately, one day the phone in her office rang and a voice said, "Is that the Headteacher?"

"Speaking," said Anne.

"I am a solicitor. You should soon be getting a divorce from your husband."

"I'm sorry," said Anne. "There are no plans for that at the moment." Then she heard giggling. She realised that it was a hoax and the giggling was from Jessica. She put down the phone.

Robert kept his promise to accompany her on part of the journey, but he made it clear that he wanted to spend his weekends away from home. Anne therefore continued to go to Jeremy in Coventry.

Suddenly Robert seemed to lose interest in accompanying her on the train. He said he needed to visit other offices. He suggested that she did drive to the school after all. Anne did this but had to set out earlier. Robert still appeared at Beaumont in the evening during the week.

One day at school she was going to be late home due to a Governing Body Meeting. She had forgotten to mention this to Robert, so she rang London University Computing Service and asked to speak to him. A man answered the phone.

"I'm sorry but he doesn't work here anymore," he said.

"I don't understand," Anne gasped. "May I speak to a Manager?"

Another man came onto the phone.

"I don't understand," stated Anne. "Robert has been leaving for work every day and returning to me in the evening. But someone says he no longer works for you."

"He doesn't, I dismissed him," was the terse reply.

"But why?" asked Anne.

"He wasn't doing what he was supposed to do. He was not getting work completed," came the answer.

"When did this happen?" enquired Anne.

"Three weeks ago, I'm sorry. Goodbye." The manager put down the phone.

Once again Anne felt shattered. For three weeks he hadn't been to work. He had not mentioned this to her at all. She had no idea. Where had he been and what had he been doing?

She managed to get through the Governing Body Meeting, but drove home very worried and upset. Robert was there.

"I have today been told that you have been dismissed from your job and have not been at work for three weeks," exclaimed Anne.

"I have found another job with ICL," stated Robert, "and start next week. I have been applying for another job for some time. I was offered a very good job at ICL, but got such a rotten reference, I didn't quite get the job I wanted."

"But what were you doing today?" asked Anne.

"If you must know I bought Jessica a new coat and some shoes. I have been spending the time with her."

Anne again felt shattered. How deceitful he was. All this had been going on and she had no knowledge of it at all. How many more times could he let her down and how many more times could she survive the hurt? She had obtained two Headships, but now she wished she could turn back the clock to be back in Kenilworth, be with Jeremy, and only 40 miles from her parents instead of 140 miles.

Anne couldn't believe that she had seen no evidence of Robert not being at work. But she had not. Then she reflected and she remembered that he had said the blue Cortina had been hit by a lorry and appeared with a red Corsair. She had just assumed that the Company had given him an alternative car. Now she realised that when he lost his job he would have also lost the Company car. He must have bought the red Corsair himself. It did look very second-hand and old.

She managed to survive all the problems with Robert by concentrating on her school. The journeys and school took up each weekday. Friday night was gardening (or Saturday morning) and then she travelled to Coventry to see Jeremy. It was too busy a life to spend a long time worrying about Robert.

CHAPTER 36

The Deputy Head of the Richmond school, Mr Shawcross, was apparently a good skier. He suggested planning a school trip to a ski resort. Anne could not ski, but loved the idea. Forty of the older children signed up for this through their parents. The destination was to be in France. La Feclaz. The ratio of care had to be, then, one to ten children. That meant there needed to be four adults at least. There was Mr Shawcross and herself; the welfare assistant volunteered, but no parent. Anne decided to ask Robert if he would assist.

In the very early days of her teaching career, before she became a Deputy Head, she had invited some of the children who seemed deprived, to her home in Kenilworth and taken them by boat into the river at Warwick. Robert then had always been kind to the children who had a great time. She of course had the permission of their parents.

Robert seemed very enthusiastic. He too liked the idea of skiing.

Everything was booked for the February half term holiday. Mr Shawcross said that by Easter the snow could be poor, so it must occur at half term. The money was collected by the School Secretary, the trip booked through Hourmont Travel. The equipment was going to be hired in La Feclaz, plus ski lessons and lift passes were arranged. It was all very exciting.

Anne purchased a white ski suit by going up to London and shopping at Lillywhites. Robert had some boating gear that he thought would suffice.

One week before the trip Robert suddenly said that he couldn't go on the trip. "We have launches for computers in France, Spain and Germany," he said. "I am too involved with these and must attend."

Anne didn't know what to think. Was it yet another excuse? Who could take his place at such short notice? She suddenly thought of Jeremy. She phoned him.

"Can you possibly get time from work to accompany us on the ski trip to La Feclaz?" she begged. Could you get the time from work?"

"I think so," countered Jeremy. "I get on well with all the management and Christine will look after Anthony I am sure."

"What about a passport?" enquired Anne.

"I went to Austria years ago with Ruby, my first and only girlfriend before Christine. I have kept it up to date. That's no problem."

"What about clothing?" worried Anne.

"Some of my mates have been skiing; they will lend me something. Don't worry."

"We shall be going to Gatwick by coach, and we will be in the entrance at 11am. Anne gave him the date and all the details.

On the day of the trip, everyone going left on the coach from the school. The Deputy Head and Welfare were with the children, but Anne drove to the airport as it was fairly close to her home. After parking the car she walked into the airport. All the children were there and Jeremy stood a way off alone. He was there, however. Anne explained to Mr Shawcross that Robert had work commitments, but she had managed to persuade a parent from a previous school to take his place. This was true in essence of course.

They all arrived safely in La Feclaz and a coach took them all to be fitted out with skis, poles and boots. The hotel was excellent and obviously used to school parties. After settling in, they all went to their rooms. By chance Jeremy's room was next to Anne's. There was an outside balcony. He could climb over a rail and get into her room through a French Door. He did this at night. Anne thought it very romantic. Not quite Romeo and Juliet, or Rapunzel, but she was delighted.

During the day they had been careful to appear very professional. Jeremy was acting as if he was another member of staff, but now here was romance. Anne's bed was slightly larger than a single bed, although it was a single room. They cuddled up together happily. In the early morning Jeremy just stepped over onto her balcony and into his room and a new day commenced.

The ski lessons were excellent. The children were soon on the ski lift within two days and they all took to the skiing well. Anne had trouble at first in turning left, but went out on her own when everyone was inside and mastered it. They were not doing parallels, but snow ploughed around. The children took to the sport so well. At the end of the week they all gained their 1st class Silver Medal. Jeremy enjoyed the sport but did not manage it quite so well. He had a weak left foot from a childhood injury. This seemed to impede him. He had no limp, so Anne thought it mainly psychological.

All the children were well and happy. Anne had given out their pocket money every morning at breakfast, so that they were able to buy souvenirs to take home from the small village shops. The week soon passed. The coach took them all to the airport and back to Gatwick. Jeremy and Anne had maintained the same professional aloofness as at the beginning, but were of course in bed together every night. Anne had already arranged when she would see him again in Coventry.

Jeremy drove home from Gatwick to Coventry and Anne to Godalming. Mr Shawcross and the Welfare Assistant were on the coach back to Richmond.

Anne was thrilled that all the children had obtained 1st Class Silver, but her thoughts were on the nights. It was the most romantic thing she had ever encountered. The lover entering by climbing over a balcony rail, onto her balcony and into her room. They had been able to whisper together about the day's events, but it was also quite a strain pretending not to be the intimate couple that they were.

Anne remembered how she nearly broke the code of secrecy. Jeremy was helping her on with her ski boot, when, without thinking, she bent down and stroked his head. He had just looked up, smiled and moved away just in time before it was noticed.

Robert was back at the house and Anne relayed to him how wonderful it was to ski. She too had obtained 1st class silver, which consisted of a small signed card as well as the medal. Robert said he was going to read up on skiing and appeared to wish that he had been there. He didn't mention his firm's launches, so whether they had really existed Anne did not know.

CHAPTER 37

Anne went to Coventry the next weekend, but the following week there was to be a social in the Church Hall for the parents of children at the school. All the staff of course were to attend. Anne had to explain to Jeremy that she must obviously be there. It was to be a dance as well, with music provided by one of the parents on some disco equipment. There was food and drink provided by the Parents Association. Anne had asked Robert to be present for appearances' sake. A big mistake.

One of her staff was an attractive lady. Young with long brown curly hair. She came up to Robert and invited him to dance. There was no alcohol available, but Robert appeared as if he had been drinking. He has driven here almost drunk, thought Anne worriedly. Robert and Miss Wilkens danced but soon Robert had his head on her shoulder and she did not seem to object. Everyone present, particularly those not dancing, noticed. The caretaker looked pityingly at Anne. She could do nothing. They were making quite a spectacle of themselves, then stayed chattering after the dance. Anne carried on as if he was not there and made sure that everyone was having a pleasant time. The social finished at 11pm and the Parents Association cleared up. Anne went back to her office after bidding people goodnight; Robert followed.

Anne was furious. "How dare you let me down at my place of work like that," she stormed. "Don't you ever dare to do such a thing to me again. Your behaviour was disgraceful."

Robert did look shamefaced. "How are you going to drive home?" she asked. "You have obviously been drinking."

"I have sobered up," countered Robert.

"I have to drive home now, but you should not be driving," Anne stated. Anne got into her car and drove home. Robert did not appear, so she guessed he had gone to Jessica's flat in London (hopefully by train). Maybe that is how he had arrived. She had just assumed that he had driven and would be driving back to Godalming. She had been inside the school, however, and not witnessed his arrival.

There was another Governing Body Meeting at the school the next week and concerns were raised about the school being very close to a main road.

The school was an old Victorian solidly-built brick building, surrounded by a large playground area at the front and rear of the school. It was enclosed with high railings. To cheer up the building Anne had encouraged one of the parents to paint large flowers on the walls. This provided quite a dramatic effect.

The managers were worrying about the future of the school as it was so close to the busy main road. Anne felt concerned that this was déjà vu.

She had noticed an advertisement for a Headteacher in a school near to the Twickenham Rugby Ground. It was a more populated school, that is, more children. She decided to apply. Again she was invited for interview, so went to see the school. It was in very nice grounds, with a large grass area edged with trees. The present Headteacher showed her around the school. He was retiring but obviously loved the school. Anne was very impressed.

She told Robert that she was applying for the position and told him when it was the day of her interview. Anne was at the school at 6 o'clock. She had had little to eat as she had had a busy day at her present school. She had told no one at the school that she had an interview for another position.

She was shown into a room, where to her amazement were six men. She was the only woman invited for interview. The interviews were being held in the school hall and at a quick peep it seemed as if there were at least 12 people there. It appeared as if the interview was going to be quite an ordeal. There was no one to offer refreshments to pass the time, and all the candidates seemed rather on edge.

All of the candidates were existing Headteachers, it emerged from very stilted conversation. One Headteacher was in the same Borough as the school and the other men seemed to have travelled from the Midlands or the North. One candidate said that his wife was waiting for him in a hotel in London.

It was a very strained and difficult situation. Seven would be hopefuls for the job of Headteacher at this obviously prestigious school. Everyone was obviously tense. The interviews did not commence until 7pm. One candidate took to walking up and down the corridor. They were called in in alphabetical order. Anne was third to be called in.

At least one of the interviewing panel smiled at her and this made her feel more relaxed. She realised that she was still wearing the camel coat in which she had driven to the school.

The panel asked questions about her career. They wanted to know what changes she would make if offered the position. Anne stated that she would prefer tables and chairs rather than the desks already in the classrooms. This would make it easier for group work and discussions. One thing she had not liked when looking round the school was a mobile hut, set apart, for children with Special Needs. It was referred to as 'The dummies' hut!' She stated that she would immediately dispense with this and would integrate the children into the other classes in their correct age range. She stated that she would form a Parent Teacher Association, as none existed at present. She also added that she would encourage music in the school. She herself could teach recorder and clarinet if necessary, and would encourage peripatetic teachers for the violin and viola.

One interviewer asked how she would cope with the journey from Godalming to this school which was in Hounslow.

"I have already done the journey many times from my home to Richmond," she replied.

The interview ended. It had lasted for 45 minutes. All of the interviews seemed to be long. The last interview ended at 11.15pm. There was a long wait. Anne went into the existing Head's room and phoned her house. She needed some comfort, some reassurance. It was such a fraught situation. There was no answer from her house. She phoned again a few minutes later. Still no reply. It was now 11.45pm. She returned to the room where all the candidates were still waiting. All were becoming more and more anxious and worried about getting home.

The door opened and her name was called. She returned to the hall where the interview had taken place. Presumably it was the Chair who spoke. "We would like to offer you the position." They confirmed that they would put this in writing and that she would start the new school year as the new Head.

"This is a plum school," stated one of the panel.

Anne thanked them. She did not know what happened to the other six candidates, as she went straight to her car and drove home. She got home at 1am. Robert was not there. She felt drained. Tired, not really hungry, but desperate for a cup of tea. She was drinking this when Robert walked in.

"How did you get on?" he asked.

"I was offered the position," replied Anne.

"I thought you'd get the job," was all that Robert said. No enquiries about the interview, no questions about other candidates. Certainly no congratulations. Anne was too weary, so went to bed.

The next day she decided to say nothing to the staff, or Vicar about her new job. There were several months to go, so she just carried on as usual.

Chapter 38

That night Robert appeared to wish to make amends for his behaviour at her school social.

"There is a dance at ICL," he proffered. "It is next Friday night. Would you like to go?"

Anne did wonder if he expected her to refuse and say that she would rather go to Coventry. It may be just another cunning ruse to stay away from home. Anne loved to dance. She and Robert had been to dancing classes in his last year at university. This was in the second year of their engagement. Robert had been an excellent dancer, picking up intricate steps then, in the Quick Step, the Foxtrot and the Tango. She hadn't learned so quickly, and sometimes the dancing master had had to go over the steps with her. However, she loved the whole ambience of dancing.

"Yes, I will come," she proffered.

Robert did not seem very pleased. Maybe as she feared it was just a placatory gesture.

She left early after school the next day and went into Dickens and Jones. There was an abundance there of lovely evening dresses. Some were phenomenally expensive. She searched for something in a less expensive price range and found a lovely blue and silver dress in her size. She tried it on. It shimmered in the light and the blue stripes on the silver background looked stunning. It had a matching blue sash and she found similar colour ribbon to tie back her hair. She already had evening shoes from her mother's shop. She drove happily back from Richmond to her home.

Friday evening came. On this occasion Robert drove her to school. She had her new dress and accessories with her. He said that he would pick her up at 7 o'clock. She could easily fill the time because there was so much to do at school, before getting herself ready for the dance.

Robert came at 7 o'clock, but spent a long time changing into his dinner suit that he had with him. Anne had actually bought this for him from Marks and Spencer years ago, when they had attended a dance at Armstrong Whitworths, his first job; he was still the same weight as was she.

Robert seemed reluctant to leave, but the caretaker was closing the school. The caretaker smiled and said, "Madam, you look lovely." He was old fashioned, but such a sweet soul.

Robert drove her to the building where the dance was being held. Anne had really no idea where she was. After parking the car, he showed her into a large room. He introduced her to some people, but she could not remember all the names. Some people were already dancing in this room and a man came up to her and asked her to dance. Anne had no idea who he was, but she politely agreed. As he was dancing with her, the man who introduced himself only as Simon, said, "Your husband must be a very worried man."

"I'm sorry," puzzled Anne. "I don't know what you mean."

"Maybe not," said Simon. He said no more and the dance came to an end.

Anne returned to Robert. "What did that man called Simon mean? He said that you must be a very worried man?"

"He was drunk," replied Robert. "Take no notice."

"My superior and his wife don't dance. They are sitting outside in the corridor. Come and be introduced."

Robert led her from the room and introduced her to his superior, Mr Gordon, and his charming wife. The passage was lined with settees and sofas, so Anne sat down and Mr Gordon's wife chatted to her.

"There is a disco in the main ballroom," Mrs Gordon stated. "But I'm afraid that the music is too loud for me."

Anne noticed that Robert had vanished. She didn't like to get up to see where he had gone, but could faintly hear the music from the disco. There seemed to be two areas for dancing, the one in which she had been and the disco.

Mrs Gordon explained, "One area is for the golden oldies like myself, and the other for the younger people. I have a bad hip, however, and cannot dance at all at the moment. I am going to have a hip replacement."

Anne sat with the Gordons for three hours and then Robert appeared. Mrs Gordon tactfully said nothing, but Anne guessed that he had been at the disco.

Robert then suggested that they left. Anne said goodnight to the Gordons and they headed for the door. By the door there suddenly appeared three girls. They all appeared young, petite with brown hair. Almost like three brown mice, thought Anne. One of them stared at Anne and then moved to almost block Robert's exit. He appeared to take no notice. They went to the car and Robert drove home.

"Why did you ask me to go?" queried Anne bitterly. "You did not dance with me once and just left me sitting in the passage with the Gordons. I would rather not have gone. I was so thrilled when I found this lovely dress and was actually looking forward to going."

"I am guessing that you invited Jessica as well and was dancing with her in the disco. I am also guessing that one of those girls by the exit was she. I didn't really take much notice, but I bet it was the one staring at me."

Robert refused to answer, so Anne guessed that she was right. Every time Robert let her down, so why was she always hurt and surprised? The next day Robert drove off and she went to Coventry.

The next week the Vicar said that he had heard of her appointment to the school in Hounslow. Anne conceded this to be the case and said that she would obviously be leaving at the end of the school year. She realised that she would have to inform the whole staff and this she did.

CHAPTER 39

On Monday Robert told her that he had to go to a Computer Conference. He was going to be away for the rest of the week. Anne felt that this could be true.

She was at home on her own on the Thursday evening when there was a knock at the front door. She opened the door and there stood a Police Officer in uniform.

"I am here to serve a summons, Madam, does your husband live here?"

"He is away in Paris at the moment," said Anne.

"Well, please give him this. It is for drink driving and he will be required to attend court."

The Police Officer gave her a large envelope. He left.

Anne was confused. She didn't open the envelope but wondered when this had taken place. She wasn't too surprised, because she was sure he was over the limit when he attended her school social. She had the feeling that he had taken to drinking too much and too frequently. They had no alcohol in the Beaumont house, however; when they were there they mainly drank coffee, as this had always been Robert's favourite drink.

Anne was upset. She phoned Robert's father for advice. He was very successful and was now a Director of his Company, previously being a Works Manager. He was obviously concerned, but could not really help. He just told her to wait until Robert returned.

Robert came back on Friday night.

"Where did this occur?" asked Anne.

"I was driving on the Hog's back," he explained. "I realised I was being followed and guessed it was an unmarked Police Car. I tried to outrun it, so I was speeding as well."

Anne realised that the Police must have caught up with him, breathalysed him and informed him that he was guilty of drink driving and speeding. He had kept this to himself. Knowing Robert, Anne thought, he hoped it would all go away. An ostrich burying its head in the sand.

Robert did not say why or when he was on the Hog's back, and Anne was too upset to enquire further. She realised that he would have to pay a fine and also lose his licence. This would certainly curtail his activities.

Interviews were held for the appointment of a new Head at her present school. Anne made sure that there were refreshments for the candidates and stayed after school to serve these herself. She did not wish anyone to go through the harrowing experience that she and others had endured at the Hounslow school. Unfortunately, no appointment was made and the position was re-advertised. New interviews were arranged and again Anne stayed to serve refreshments and to put the candidates at their ease. This time an appointment was made. A Mr Bell was appointed. Anne also had been very impressed with him and knew that the school would be in safe and capable hands.

It was soon time for her leaving Assembly. It was held in the Church Hall and many parents attended. She was presented with a silver cake stand and some crystal goblets. The Vicar thanked her for her services and she made a short speech of thanks, and stated how much she had enjoyed her stay at the school and that it had been a privilege to be the Headteacher of such an excellent establishment. The most poignant moment for her was with the caretaker, Mr Simms.

He wept, and said how much he had valued working with her. He was such a gentle soul and had tried assiduously to please. Anne knew that she would not meet his like again. There had been a husband and wife team as caretakers at her first teaching school, and they had behaved as if they were characters out of a Charles Dickens novel. Anne thanked him profusely for all that he had done. The term ended and she drove away sadly.

CHAPTER 40

During the summer holidays, Anne did go camping with Jeremy and his sons. Jeremy was well organised with a Calor Gas Stove and provisions. It was a ridge tent with an awning. She bought a sleeping bag and brought with her an inflatable boat that had originally been purchased by Robert at Kenilworth. They were camping at Durdle Door, near to Lulworth in Dorset. Durdle Door beach she knew was one of the most amazing beaches in Dorset and she thought the inflatable boat could be enjoyed on the sea by the boys.

The holiday went well. They did visit Lulworth Cove which is a great beauty spot. The boys swam in the sea and Anne helped with the cooking. She also bought groceries from a mobile shop on site. All went well until William decided to do handstands on the inflatable boat. It caught on some sharp rock on the seabed and punctured. The boat obviously collapsed. William dragged it from the water. Jeremy tried to repair it, with a puncture repair kit that he had, but it was useless. Anne was not annoyed. She was just sorry that the boys' enjoyment had been curtailed.

The next day they went into Weymouth and Anne purchased another inflatable similar to the previous one. It was the penultimate day of the holiday. Anne presumed that as she had brought the now ruined boat with her, she would be taking back this new one. Suddenly, Jeremy's mood changed as had happened in the early days of their relationship.

"What are you going to do with that boat?" he snapped.

"Well, I shall take it back and hopefully we can use it on another occasion."

"How selfish can you be? Why haven't you offered it to the boys?" Jeremy almost seemed to snarl.

Anne felt that it was too late now to say anything. She knew from years ago, that when Jeremy got into this kind of mood, it was hopeless. All that evening Jeremy refused to speak to her. He walked off on his own, leaving the boys to play at football. When he returned, they had a meal, but Jeremy was curt and unsociable. Anne, as she had many times before when he was with his children, felt an outsider.

The next day they packed up, and left in their two cars. Jeremy drew up at Winchester and Anne stopped also. There was a river nearby and they all got out to walk beside it. Anne suddenly couldn't stop crying. All the stress and grief from her life seemed to pour out. All the problems she had with Robert and the fact that she felt Jeremy had never truly loved her. She knew that it was a difficult situation for him. The boy's mother, sweet as she was, was now living with another man. But she felt that however hard she had tried, she had never really felt included whether he was with both boys, or just Anthony.

She sobbed and sobbed, Jeremy just walked ahead with the boys. She returned to her car. Jeremy did return and said almost sarcastically, "Well you go one way, and I go the other." Anne drove home, and once again felt miserable and unhappy. She felt like a piece of dandelion clock floating in the wind, but there was nothing stable for her.

CHAPTER 41

T he next week was the commencement of her new job. There was a lovely office with a huge wooden desk, an adjoining room with a wash basin and mirror and her own private toilet.

Assembly was at five past nine. Hymn books were available for the children and as there seemed no proficient pianist on the staff, Anne played for the hymn. She told the children a story with a moral and wished them all well in the new school year. A new life here had begun.

There was to be a welcoming social for the parents to volunteer for a PTA. A letter had been sent out on her first day at the school. There was an excellent Secretary. The Welfare Assistant purchased the refreshments from an existing School Fund and before the general social there was an initial meeting to nominate and second, parents for the PTA Committee. Their names were taken down by the attending Secretary. After the more formal meeting, there was a general social interaction. Anne had of course introduced herself to the parents and put forward some of her plans for the school.

People were chatting and laughing and enjoying the refreshments of sausage rolls, vol-au-vents and finger sandwiches.

Suddenly, Anne noticed Robert in the doorway of the hall. She slipped out, ushered him into her office and asked him what was wrong.

After purchasing the red Ford Corsair, Robert had changed this for a Lotus Europa. It was a great design and a super car. This had been the car in which Robert had tried to outrun the Police before he was stopped.

"I've smashed the car," he stated. "The sun was in my eyes and I hit a wall. It has had to be towed away. I have walked from the tube station and need a lift home."

Anne went back to the Social which was closing down now. Members of the newly formed PTA Committee cleared away into a small kitchen opposite the Secretary's office. Rubbish was bagged up and chairs put away. Parents gradually left.

Anne made Robert a coffee before they left in her car. She now had a TR7 which she had collected from a garage in Coventry when visiting Jeremy. She had traded in her Ford Capri for her present car. The TR7 at this time was produced at a factory in Coventry. She drove Robert home.

"I have had a date for my appearance in court," he said. "I shall get the Lotus repaired and I shall swop it then for an MGB sports car that I have seen. The Lotus was a great car, but the wheels kept dropping off."

Anne was flabbergasted. Did he live in a real world? Here he was talking blithely about another car. He had just smashed the Europa, what damage she did not know, and soon he would almost certainly be banned from driving.

"When is the court case?" enquired Anne.

"In three weeks' time."

"Do you not realise that you will almost certainly be banned from driving?"

"Maybe not," replied Robert, yet again with his head in the sand. "I am still going to buy the MGB. It looks a smashing car."

Anne was too tired again to argue with him. She went to bed.

Robert got the Lotus repaired and then nothing could stop him from eventually buying the MGB. It was a lovely colour, a bright yellowish lime green. Anne rather liked it for herself, but of course she had the TR7 collected from the factory in Coventry when she last visited Jeremy.

The court day for Robert arrived and as Anne had anticipated, he was banned from driving for a year and had to pay a fine.

Robert's office had now moved to Putney. "How will you get to work?" enquired Anne.

"I can come with you," countered Robert. "I can easily walk to Hounslow tube station from your school. No problem."

"How will you get home at night?" asked Anne.

"Again, I shall walk to the school from the tube station."

"How will I know what time you are coming?" worried Anne.

"Well, you are always late. Sorting out invoices, ordering stock, or putting up art work in the entrance hall. Shall we say 7.30pm?"

"What if there is a PTA meeting?"

"Well I shall just have to wait in your office."

Anne wondered if this would all work out. Once he would have stayed with Jessica, but she had obviously got tired of waiting. Robert had told Anne a while ago, that she had met a pharmacist, who had a very wealthy father. Robert had told her because he was upset at first. Apparently, he had gone to her flat (for which he was paying), and this guy was there. Jessica introduced Robert to the young man, whose name was Julian. She had passed off the incident stating that Robert was just a 'father figure'. Jessica was, so he said, soon to be married. They were in the flat at the moment, but were going to move to a riverside house in Sunbury.

Robert now had no immediate place to stay in London, so Anne thought perhaps the arrangement he mentioned would work out despite her misgivings.

CHAPTER 42

A flyer had arrived at the school advertising a Diploma in Education from the Maria Grey College between Twickenham and Isleworth. Anne only had her Teaching Certificate from Birmingham University, although she trained at Leicester. She felt that she should have additional qualifications. She decided to apply and was accepted. Hounslow Council were very good. They allowed her to have a half day from school. The Council also paid for her tuition and books.

Anne started this as it was fairly immediate. She had to be back at school to take Robert home at 7.30pm on the college day.

She was very busy. She was driving to school each day, going to college on Tuesday afternoons, waiting for Robert until 7.30pm and sometimes studying or writing essays until midnight.

Robert now had nowhere to go at weekends. He said that he would go to his parents in Carshalton. He added that his father was having heart problems, so he felt he should spend time with him. He said that he would go straight from work on Fridays and return by train and bus on Sunday.

Anne managed to complete her essays late at night and visited Jeremy on Saturdays. He mentioned that he had met a lady at a Singles Club, and he was driving her home plus some of her friends afterwards. It didn't seem serious and Anne felt that their now long relationship was on terra firma.

One thing she had noticed when at the Beaumont house were some silent phone calls. These seemed to be exacerbating. She would pick up the phone and say her usual "Hello". Then there was silence. She was sure that she could hear someone breathing, but there was silence. It was she that first put the phone down. This got so irritating that one day she expostulated, "Who are you? Would you please speak? What is your name?" One answer came "Mary Smith" and the phone went down. Anne realised that it was a pseudonym, but also that it had previously been a female caller.

Robert had some news. "I have taken another flat. Jessica is married to Julian and that flat has been re-let. The flat I have is well appointed and I was fortunate to find it."

"So you won't need a lift in the morning or come to school in the evening?"

"Well it's only until I get my licence back. It is rather inconvenient. I am tired of walking to and from the tube station. I shall stay at the flat in the week. You can get home earlier sometimes and work on your Diploma."

Anne was not really surprised to hear this. "May I see the flat?" she asked.

"Sure! We will go there tomorrow after school. I am not occupying it for another week, but I'm sure the owner will let you see it."

The next night Robert directed Anne to the flat. They were allowed in. It was lovely. Meticulously clean and well furnished.

"You are lucky," stated Anne, but she hesitated to ask what the rent was per month.

Robert took over the tenancy of the flat for the remainder of the year. It seemed now as if they were really separated. She did not see him during the week and sometimes did not hear from him at all during the weekend.

She decided to drive to Coventry in Robert's MGB one day, as it was left standing solitary in her garage. The car went well and it actually seemed quite fun to drive a different car. It had plenty of petrol, so she did not have to stop.

Jeremy had started to build a boat in his conservatory. When built it could be removed through the rear of his garden and the side entrance to his house. It was going to be a motorboat. Anne had to admit that he was gifted. He seemed to have no specifications and just seemed to be building it from a plan in his head. It was already taking shape. Jeremy said that the guys at work were helping him, by obtaining parts for him. They still managed, however, to go out on Saturday evenings and on Sunday Anne drove home. She didn't know if Robert would be there, but he was.

She agreed to take him straight to work on the Monday, which she did.

Instead of thanking her, however, he said, "You only drove me here to spy on me." No thanks, no goodbye, just an exit. Anne drove to school and felt that with Robert she would never win. All the time he had stayed at Beaumont house he had still made no financial contribution whatsoever. He wouldn't now of course, because he was soon to be in his flat.

The same pattern emerged. School, home study and going to Jeremy at the weekend. Anne always had that feeling of perhaps fear as she drove home towards the house on Sunday. Would she see the lights on, and Robert would be there or not? It was a horrible feeling, the not knowing. Sometimes he was there, and she drove him to work or sometimes he was not. If he was not, he explained later that he had had to go abroad for work, but he never told her in advance where or when he was going.

It was time for the Diploma in Education examinations. They were actually set by the University of London. Hounslow Education Authority gave her leave for study.

Anne contacted Jeremy. "I really need to study and cannot come to Coventry for a month. Hounslow are giving me a week's leave, but I need the preceding weekends as well. I will ring you at the end of the month."

Robert did not appear. Anne just concentrated on her school and her studies. One of her studies was of Jean Jacques Rousseau (1712 – 1778), a Swiss born philosopher, also The Arts in Schools by the Calouste Gulbenkian Foundation. Their mantra was that the arts have an essential place in Education. Anne had much enjoyed reading these and other philosophers.

The exams went well and Anne felt confident. She learned fairly quickly that she had passed. She could now put Dip. Ed (Lond) after her name. She phoned Jeremy. "I can come to see you again," she said excitedly.

Jeremy had a strange story. Not about the lady at the Singles Club, but, it seemed, another.

"I was in a restaurant," he said, "and met this lady. We got talking and now we are seeing each other regularly."

Anne was stunned.

He added, "You need to get on with your life. You always seem to be successful."

Anne tried, "So you don't want me to come up? I have only been studying and taking my examinations."

"I know," said Jeremy. "But I have to get on with my life as well. Take care." He rang off.

That is that, thought Anne. He had waited a long time for her. He had sent William to his mother when she was at Kenilworth and she always believed that he hoped she would take Anthony and himself into her home there. He had suggested moving his job to Dunsfold, so that he could come with Anthony to Beaumont. She had never suggested a permanent commitment.

She had forged ahead with her career. She mused that this had been Robert's criticism of her in the initial divorce proceedings. That she was too dedicated to teaching.

CHAPTER 43

It was time to change the TR7. There was a different model out with a roof that slid back. These were still being made in Coventry. She was doing a part exchange and needed to pick the car up. She wrote to Jeremy and asked if she could call in when she collected the car. He phoned her back and said that if she drove up on the Friday evening he would be there. This she did. Jeremy seemed his old self. He was still a handsome man and Anne certainly cared for him. He had been her saviour, when she was at rock bottom and perhaps she had done the same for him. She couldn't really believe that it was all over.

She went into the house. Jeremy immediately stroked her face and led her upstairs to his bedroom. Anthony was obviously out. They made love as they had done many, many times before. Surely everything now was going to be alright again? Robert had his flat and she hardly ever saw him. She needed Jeremy for emotional support.

Jeremy suddenly got out of the bed. "I have to meet Charmaine," he said. "Make yourself at home. I will be back later." He dressed quickly and left. Anne did not know what to do. She used his phone and phoned her parents. Not to tell them of these events, but to say that she was picking up a new car and would be driving over probably on Saturday or Sunday. She told them about the Diploma and her father particularly was delighted.

Jeremy came back at about midnight. As usual he slept with his arm around her. Anthony had not appeared so she assumed that he must be with his mother.

In the morning Anne didn't know what to expect.

"Anthony is permanently with his mother now," stated Jeremy. "What are you going to do today?"

"I have to pick up my new car," replied Anne.

"Well, I have promised to take Charmaine to the Baginton Air Show," said Jeremy. "But you can come back here when you have picked up your car if you wish."

Anne realised that Jeremy was indeed building a new life.

"I will collect my car and go to Wellingborough," she said.

She got dressed, and they had some tea. Jeremy still hadn't put a shirt on and she thought what a fine figure of a man he was. Despite his moods and tempers, they had had some great times. Jeremy put his shirt on and Anne moved towards the door. As she got into the car, he knelt down and kissed her. Smiling sadly she drove away. This chapter seemed to be closed.

She exchanged her car and the manager at the garage gave her a huge bunch of flowers as she settled the bill.

She drove to Wellingborough to her parents. She gave her mother the flowers. Her mother made a lovely meal as usual. They all chatted afterwards. Anne just told them that Robert now had a flat and seldom came home. Her parents were not surprised. They considered Robert to be a hopeless case, although Anne secretly felt that her father had admired Robert's brain. She couldn't argue that he was not bright. He had passed the then School Certificate and gained 5 A' levels. She couldn't understand why he hadn't made Oxford or Cambridge, but knew that he would not interview well. He would be far too self-effacing and not dynamic. Strangely this didn't come through in real life. It didn't seem self-effacing then. His mother had once told her that she thought him a

Jekyll and Hyde character.

Anne stayed the night and drove back to her house the next day. Robert was there. She told him that Jeremy now had a new life. She had noticed that Jeremy's boat was nearly completed and it looked great. She told Robert that she thought Charmaine was the lady from the Singles Club and that he had known her now for quite a while. Jeremy's tale about meeting someone in a restaurant was a red herring. Anne guessed that as Charmaine had a house and being a widow, Jeremy would probably marry her. She also knew that he was longing to take his boat to Lake Windermere. Anthony was definitely with his mother. She heard that William was a PE Instructor in the army at Aldershot. After all the heartache it seemed as if Jeremy's life was back on track.

Anne decided to do some further studying. She asked for some advice from Maria Grey and they told her that she could register for a degree. Unfortunately, as her Teaching Certificate was outside London, she would have to do a qualifying year, which would still give her some points, before going onto a Bachelor of Education Course proper. She had to do this from Roehampton College. She applied and was accepted. Once again Hounslow Education Authority supported her. They allowed her to leave school on Tuesday afternoon to attend the college and then she continued to Southland College for the evening session. Hounslow paid for her tuition again, her books and even gave her a petrol allowance. They were most generous.

It was hard, still having a full-time job, taking recorder groups at lunchtime, attending and organising Management Meetings and PTA meetings. There was now a new innovation, a Governing Body. These meetings sometimes lasted until 11pm. Anne felt very bitter about these. She had been at school all day with little to eat but had to stay for the meetings. The Welfare Assistant always left tea and coffee plus sandwiches, but when the members of the Governing Body walked in, they expected her to serve them.

Anne managed to write her essays at the weekend and there were many essays to write. She had to examine and comment on previously published Education Documents from the D.E.S. She had to examine the Montessori method of Education and study Freud and the Nuffield method of Education. It was very challenging for her, but she rose to the challenge.

She did hear from Jeremy again briefly. He phoned her at school and asked if she would give him a reference to teach carpentry. He explained that he had been made redundant. Anne said that of course she would. He seemed happy. He said that he was looking for other work. He was married to Charmaine and had married in a Registry Office. He had sold his house and given half of the profit to Christine. Some of the finance for the house of course had been on a mortgage. He had moved into Charmaine's house, just as Anne had anticipated.

He didn't actually ask her to send a reference, so Anne guessed it had really only been for a vague possibility and he wished to tell her of his new situation.

CHAPTER 44

The time was coming for Robert to once again be able to drive. He said that the flat was very expensive and he would be giving it up. He said that when practical he would take her to school and pick her up at 7.30pm. She would obviously have to drive herself when there were evening functions such as PTA meetings or Governing Body Meetings. Robert added, "Driving's nothing to me."

Anne wanted to laugh. What a thing to say after he had been banned for a year. Still, she must admit, he had taught her to drive before she had driving lessons. He had passed his test the first time apparently at 17 and previously always seemed a competent driver.

He told her the story of the Hog's back fiasco at last. Whether or not it was the truth she couldn't say. His story was that ICL was sponsoring a racing driver in Formula 2 at Thruxton, near to Basingstoke. Robert said he was responsible for organising potential customers in a hospitality bus. There were snacks and drinks. He had obviously partaken a great deal of the wine himself. He was caught by the police as he was driving back. Still, that was now in the past. At last Robert was able to drive the MGB.

True to his word, he did drive Anne to school. He picked her up when possible at 7.30pm. Robert was even now helping with the garden at the weekend. The gardener had been doing a great job for a long time now. It was a big garden and required a lot of work. Anne had always planted the flowers.

Winter Pansies in the autumn and Impatiens and Begonias mainly in the spring.

She was managing her essays and the qualifying year for the degree was progressing well. It seemed a short year and soon the examinations were upon her. They were at the end of May. She felt that she had done well. She felt like celebrating.

Robert promised to pick her up at seven and said that he would take her to The Bear at Esher for a meal as a reward for all her hard work in the qualifying year.

Anne put on a white blouse and a long black skirt for the occasion. She waited. Suddenly the phone rang. It was Robert. "I can't make it," he said. "Something has come up." I am sending a Mini Cab to take you home. A Mini Cab drew into the school car park as if by magic. Anne had no choice but to grab the suit she had changed from, her bag and leave. The caretaker always locked up.

The driver did not converse but needed directions to her house. He had already been paid, he said, but as he was unsure of the direction Anne couldn't see how that could have happened. Robert must have been desperate and paid him a handsome sum in advance. Robert did not come home that night at all.

When he did come home he made no apologies or offered real reasons for his non-appearance. What he did say was that he was changing his MGB for a Jaguar. Anne was puzzled about this. The MGB was a super little car and due to his driving ban he had hardly driven it.

"I've seen this super car," he said. "Silver blue. I've always wanted a Jaguar. It is in a garage at Putney. I am trading in the MGB."

Anne wondered if he wished to impress a new girlfriend with a more prestigious car. She was now used to his machinations.

Within days he brought the silver blue Jaguar to Beaumont House. It did look spectacular. Robert was driving to work in it on his own, however, because he said he had so many other people to visit. He said that they were connected to exhibitions for the computers, such as graphic designers and designers for stands.

Anne drove herself to and from school, until one day once again he appeared at her school in the evening minus the car.

"What has happened this time?" enquired Anne, already bracing herself for more trouble.

"I hit a parking meter with the car. The side is caved in. I had to get it towed away. The garage can give me no timeline when it will be repaired."

"Are you claiming on the insurance?" asked Anne.

"I suppose so. I would like it fixed quickly; however, the Assessors for Insurance take ages. The garage have said they will have to find a new door and that will take time. I just can't believe it has happened."

"How did it occur?" asked Anne.

"The sun got in my eyes again. I also got rather blocked in with traffic. The road was very busy."

Anne sighed. Always excuses, never his fault. But here he was, wanting a lift home.

CHAPTER 45

Once again Anne was driving Robert to her school and he was walking to the tube station. She wasn't going to drive him to Putney again and be accused of 'spying'. At night she would wait for him in her office for him to appear. He came a couple of times, but one night she waited and waited and he did not come.

The Deputy Head, Mr Garrow, was still in the school. Anne had been putting some art work onto pin boards in the Entrance Hall and had not realised that he was still there. The previous Headmaster had eulogised about this teacher, stating how dedicated he was to the school. Indeed, he had always been supportive in all her new ventures, such as the opening up of classrooms, the exit of the old desks and purchase of new tables and chairs into every classroom. He was obviously an excellent teacher and an invaluable asset to the school. She felt that he had waited at the school and not gone home because she was still there. Perhaps he had done this before, but maybe he had stayed in his classroom and she hadn't noticed.

Anne still waited. There was no word from Robert. Mr Garrow came into her office.

"It's very late, Mrs Deighton. Are you waiting for your husband?" (He had obviously noticed the previous appearances of Robert.)

Anne was feeling upset. "Yes, but he hasn't turned up. He had damaged his car and I have been driving him home.

I don't think he is coming tonight, however." Anne then confessed, "I am afraid that things have not been well with us for many years."

Mr Garrow then surprised her by saying, "Mr Smith on the staff saw your husband going into a hotel with a dark-haired girl on several occasions in Chiswick. Mr Smith told the staff, but of course we said nothing to you. Mr Smith thought they looked very familiar together. I had the feeling that all was not well. Come, it is time for you to go home. Have you eaten?"

"No," said Anne. "But will your wife not wonder where you are?"

"That is another story," countered Mr Garrow. "We had two houses and my wife preferred the house in the Cotswolds. She wanted me to move there, but I wished to stay in Isleworth near to the school. We separated and that was that. There is more to this story, however, that I may tell you another day. I will ride shotgun behind you, and we will pick up some fish and chips in Twickenham."

"Thank you so much," said Anne gratefully, but still wondering where Robert was.

Anne drove out of the gates and at Twickenham they both stopped and Mr Garrow picked up fish and chips. They drove on until they came to a wooded parking area. Anne got out of her car and into Mr Garrow's car. They ate the fish and chips.

"My tale is rather a sad one," proffered Mr Garrow. "I was called up for World War Two, but because of my qualifications from the City of London School (my father was a Headmaster), I went to Sandhurst and became an Officer. I had previously met a teacher who was older than myself, but I promised to marry her when she told me that she had had to have an abortion. When the war was over, I honoured my promise, but we were totally unsuited. I fell in love with another teacher who was Roman Catholic. She refused to let me break my marriage vows, but we were very much in love. Sadly, she got pancreatic cancer and died."

"That is a very sad story," said Anne. "My tale of woe is too long to tell. But I must be getting home otherwise I shall be too tired for school tomorrow. Thank you so much for your concern." Anne went to her own car and drove home.

Robert came home by taxi at about midnight. He just said that he was so busy with the launch of a new computer. He did not explain why he had not phoned. He still went with Anne as far as the school the next day.

Anne was concerned. Was this going to be a new pattern of behaviour for Robert? She wondered what was now in Robert's mind. There always seemed to be so many twists and turns in his behaviour.

Anne again waited after school for Robert to arrive. She went down to the school library and rearranged some books that the children returned with their teacher into alphabetical order. The children often made mistakes when putting their books back onto the shelves. They would indent them under the initial letter of the first name of the author instead of the last name. All of the children in the school were allowed to borrow two books per week and went into the library under the guidance of their Class Teacher.

Anne returned to her office. The time was getting on. Once again it was eight o'clock. Anne had an 'open door' policy unless something serious occurred. Mr Garrow again popped his head around the door and then came in.

"No show?" he queried.

"I'm afraid not," replied Anne. "I would hate to drive off and then Robert came, however."

"Is it likely?" asked Mr Garrow.

"I suppose not," answered Anne.

"Well, shall we do the same as last evening? I will ride shotgun and then pick up the fish and chips again in Twickenham. We can park in the same position as last evening."

Anne was hungry. If Robert was going to be late, as least he could and should have phoned.

"Very well. Thank you," she said. They did exactly the same as the previous evening. When in his car Mr Garrow told her a little more about his life.

"When I married Gladys, I realised at once that we had completely different tastes. She preferred 1930s furniture and I prefer antiques. My family had many genuine antiques, including a James I chest of drawers. I love classical music, but Gladys did not. I like opera, Gladys did not. We lived in a flat when I was demobbed, but bought my house in Isleworth from inherited money when my parents died. My aunt also sadly passed away and I again inherited money. I wanted to buy a house near to the sea but Gladys would not agree. I then found a lovely house near to a Water Mill but Gladys did not approve of that. Finally we settled on a house in the countryside in Gloucestershire. My wife loved it and I employed builders to extend it, put in a new kitchen, leaded lights and an oriel window."

"I found some lovely pieces of furniture in Gloucester, including a prie-diue. It was and is charming, but Gladys continued to insist that I left the school and move there permanently. This I did not wish to do. In any case I would have been moving away from the love of my life who was on the school staff. As I told you before, sadly she died, but I still did not want to leave school and move to Gloucestershire. My wife is living there now, with our springer spaniel, Judge."

"I thought you were divorced," said Anne.

"We really are in the final process of divorce. The financial settlement is fairly straightforward. Gladys wishes to keep the Gloucestershire house and I am happy to keep the house in Isleworth. They are similar in value, Isleworth property being so near to London is usually of a higher value, but I spent a great deal of money on the Gloucestershire property. They have been valued and in value are like for like. Anyway, enough about me. Things have obviously not been good between yourself and Robert."

"I will just sum it up," replied Anne. "He left me many years ago and had several lady friends after that time I believe. He certainly left me for a girl called Marilyn, and kept another girl called Jessica in a flat for several years until she got married. He had an affair with our landlady when I moved from Kenilworth down south and had to stay temporarily in a bedsit. I am convinced that there have been others."

"This is your third Headship, I believe," stated Mr Garrow.

"Yes. My previous Headships were in Godalming, the one I moved to from Kenilworth, then one in Richmond and now this."

"Quite a career," admitted Mr Garrow. "I believe your father was only a cop."

Anne was angry. She guessed this must have been disclosed from the previous Head Teacher, who had asked her in passing, the employment of her father. He had obviously lived in an old fashioned world of a tiered class society.

Anne loved her father dearly. He had given her a wonderful childhood. Both her parents had been good to her, giving her a tricycle, small two wheeled bicycle, and when she passed the Scholarship at ten, it was her father, she was told, who purchased a three gear bicycle, carried it up the stairs and left it on the landing, sporting a big red bow for her Christmas present. They had gone on many bicycle rides together. He had made up treasure hunts for her (one treasure was an amethyst pendant on a gold chain which she did treasure). He visited her when she was at Leicester College many times.

'Only a cop'. Anne thanked Mr Garrow again and drove off. How supercilious could you be? Good luck with the prie-dieu and all the rest, she thought crossly.

Robert did not come home, and despite feeling angry with Mr Garrow, she still went with him the next night, for fish and chips again. They parked in the same place but Anne didn't stay long. Mr Garrow said that he would ride shotgun as far as Newlands Corner before Shere in Surrey, which he did. They continued in this pattern until the weekend.

CHAPTER 46

Robert's car was apparently repaired. It had been resprayed in the same colour as previously and looked perfect. Robert had an announcement. "I have taken another flat," he informed her. "I am tired of travelling from Putney to Godalming. It takes up too much time and the traffic is increasing."

"Well I have to do it," replied Anne sharply. "And have taken you as well on many occasions. Where is this flat?"

"In Wandsworth," replied Robert. This time Anne did not ask to see it. Logically it could be for both of them, so of course could the other flat he had when he lost his licence. He had never suggested that and neither had she. She had thought the first flat only a temporary arrangement and preferred to go home where all her clothes, books and computer were.

This new arrangement seemed more serious. "I may get home at weekends," offered Robert.

"Oh! Ho! Jolly good! Super Super!" thought Anne. "Am I supposed to be grateful?!"

Recently she had asked the gardener to find a painter and decorator to repaint the windows and doors and to use white outdoor emulsion for the top half of the house. It had been quite expensive, but of course Robert had made no financial contribution. She was also having to have the drive resurfaced in red tar macadam, but she knew that she would have to bear the financial cost herself. It seemed as if the Beaumont House was a kind of Posting house or Traveller's

Lodge for Robert.

She did not argue with him. It was pointless. Robert just wanted to live his own life in his own way. She did wonder, however, if he was living with someone in this Wandsworth flat. Actually, she had got used to the journey from her house to school and just accepted it. Robert obviously could not.

On Monday, she need not stay late as she knew that Robert was not coming. After school Mr Garrow came in. "Are you waiting again?" he inquired.

"No," replied Anne. "Robert is tired of the journey and has a flat now in Wandsworth. He hasn't suggested it, but I have no wish to join him there. I prefer to travel home."

Anne suddenly had a thought. Her office was comfortable, but quite mundane. A huge desk, with a revolving chair, several bookcases, a coffee table and two modern armchairs by the gas fire set into a brick fireplace. There was a golden carpet that she had had fitted in her first year as Head, and the only luxury, velvet curtains. She had purchased these herself at her previous school, and had them rehung here. She felt that Mr Garrow thought this similar to her own home. He had seemed so superior with his prie-dieu, and even mentioned all the silver he still had in his present house at Isleworth. She made a decision.

"Would you like to come to my house in Godalming? We can still have something from the chip shop, but then continue."

"I would be delighted," said Mr Garrow. This they did.

When they arrived at Beaumont House Anne quickly opened the door and put on all the lights. Mr Garrow walked into a hall that had carved antique chairs, gold mirrors and silver ornaments. She showed him into the main living room. The chandeliers gleamed with myriad candle bulbs from the ceiling. There was the Wilton carpet. Gilt mirrored tables laden with silver items. A bow window with antique china and Victorian lustres. Gilt mirrors on the walls, with antique hanging plates in place. A marble fireplace. A gold velvet three-piece suite in antique design. Wine tables with candelabra.

Mr Garrow sat on the settee. His face was almost puce. He had certainly not been expecting to see the type of furnishing that he obviously relished.

He went into the adjoining dining room. A reproduction Queen Anne dining room suite. Silver tureens on the table. A further candelabra hanging from the ceiling to name but some of the items he saw. Dark blue velvet draped curtains were at all the Georgian Windows.

Anne could see Mr Garrow's face, and she had a secret gloating, because she felt sure that he thought her home very inferior to that of his.

He did say, "It's like being in the Palace at Versailles."

Anne made him a cup of tea. Thanked him for accompanying her and he left. "Ho Ho!" thought Anne gleefully. She did realise, however, that he had been brought up in a very superior home and obviously loved antiques in the same way that she did.

Anne's Godmother had been Lady Rundle and she had seen as a child the very rare and real antique items of furniture. Her grandfather on her father's side had a home full of valuable items and these were now in her parents' home in Wellingborough. Here there was an eighteenth century corner stand that she had always loved and at Wellingborough there was a collection of very valuable Japanese hanging plates. Her taste had prevailed, but Robert was not so interested.

The next day at school, Anne noticed a change in Mr Garrow's demeanour. At lunchtime, before she went to her recorder group, he said that he had something to give her. Anne was surprised, but sat down. Mr Garrow produced three very ornate brass trays. He said that he had bought them when in Egypt. He stated that when liberating France after D-Day he was shot by a sniper. After recuperating, he was sent as an Officer onto an Interviewing Panel firstly in Egypt and then Greece. He asked if she would accept them. Anne didn't quite know what to say, but felt it churlish to refuse. She accepted them.

"Why don't we go to Ripley this evening for a meal?" Mr Garrow suggested.

Anne was not a big eater. She always remembered she had put on weight in her first year at College. The food at Humbastone College was superb. She had lodged with a Mrs Dean for bed, breakfast and evening meal as the Halls of Residence had been already full when she applied, but the lunch and afternoon tea supplied by the College were excellent. Her mother made her aware she had put on weight by saying, "You are getting broad in the beam, my girl." Anne immediately cut down on the food and missed out the afternoon tea altogether. She soon regained her former slim weight which she watched carefully.

"I did eat the fish and chips," admitted Anne, "but I don't normally eat big meals, though thank you for asking."

"I know you usually have little to eat," said Mr Garrow. "I always have a school dinner as you know, but you seem to exist all day on coffee. I am sure that I could order a salad for you, however."

Anne felt it was lovely to have someone who seemed to care for her, if only a little.

Mr Garrow appeared quite elderly for his age, which was 14 years older than Anne. Anne was now 44 so Mr Garrow must be 58 she thought. He looked older, however, because he was asthmatic and needed a Ventolin inhaler. She had learned from the previous Head that after he had been shot in France, he was quite ill after being transported by ship back to England. The bullet had apparently gone through his shoulder into his lung.

After Anne had started as Headteacher, he had been absent for several weeks with congestion of the lungs. For a long time now, however, he seemed fit and well and as said before a very supportive Deputy Head and an excellent class teacher. She knew that he had the greatest respect from parents, teachers and of course the children.

Anne was not thinking of romance. She was longing for some kindness and consideration. Neither of these were coming from Robert. He really was so terribly selfish and when he had said all those years ago, "I have not loved you for 12 years," she knew that that still held true today.

They both drove to Ripley and in the restaurant Mr Garrow had a steak pie and Anne had her salad. They talked about the impending Ofsted Inspection, that now regularly took place in a range of educational institutions. Everyone involved in this inspection was apprehensive because a bad report could be disastrous. Their inspection was due shortly.

After the meal there was a calamity. They went into the public bar and Mr Garrow had a lager and Anne had a tonic water. She knew that Mr Garrow had also applied for the Headship but he had not been shortlisted. She was chatting about her career at this point, and ended a sentence with, 'with all that I have achieved'.

Surprisingly, Mr Garrow snapped, "Well what have you achieved?"

Anne lost her temper. She was worried about Robert. She was worried about the forthcoming Ofsted Inspection and she was unclear how this present friendship was developing. She threw the remainder of the tonic water into Mr Garrow's face and walked out to her car.

Mr Garrow rushed after her. "I am so sorry," he apologised. "I cannot believe I said that. I know that you have gained three Headships, you are a talented pianist, and you have gained your Diploma in Education. I suppose a tiny bit of resentment emerged because I love the school and I was not even shortlisted."

Anne accepted his apology because she knew that she too had behaved atrociously. It was not like her to do something like that. She realised that she had been under a tremendous strain for a very long time. Fortunately it did not affect her daily school life. It had been an additional strain studying for the Diploma in Education and the qualifying year for the Bachelor of Education. She was of course continuing with this degree, but it was hard finding time for study and essays.

She thanked Mr Garrow for the meal. He was quite mortified with how the situation had deteriorated. "I will ride shotgun to Newlands Corner again," he offered. Anne nodded and drove off. Mr Garrow was behind her in his car, but turned off when they reached the road that led to Shere. Anne then had to drive across some hills on a narrow road, before reaching home. "Oh dear," she thought. "I obviously need a good night's sleep before reflecting on anything."

CHAPTER 47

The school was gearing up for the Ofsted Inspection. An Office had to be set aside for the Inspectors and food had to be provided. Luckily the school had its own canteen. All timetables had to be submitted. The day for the first visit of the Inspectors arrived. They came into the staffroom. Mr Garrow came and sat beside Anne. This felt strangely comforting.

Mr Damun, the Chief Inspector, informed the staff that members of the team would visit lessons at random. None of the staff spoke and Mr Damun lightened the atmosphere by talking about some amusing incidents in his career.

The Inspectors stayed for four days and then asked to meet Mr Garrow and herself in her office. They went through all the areas of the curriculum with comments. They had enjoyed her Assemblies, and gave the school an Outstanding Report. They stated that it was one of the best reports for a school in the South of England.

Their report would be published and of course copies sent to Hounslow Education Authority, the Governing Body and to the school. They all left after asking staff to be thanked for their hospitality and co-operation.

Anne and Mr Garrow were ecstatic. They drove in their cars to the hostelry at St Johns. Anne had a Vodka and lime and Mr Garrow a Gin and tonic. They were both so overjoyed. Mr Garrow suddenly said, "Would you like to see my home at Isleworth? We could celebrate there."

"I dare not drink too much because of driving," retorted Anne.

"You could stay the night. I have three bedrooms and a large bathroom with a shower."

Anne was so euphoric at the good result from the Inspectors, she capitulated. "Thank you," she said.

Mr Garrow's house was quite large. It was semi-detached with large bay windows and fairly close to Osterley Park. When she entered the house, Anne's first vision was of a huge Grandfather clock standing in quite a large entrance hall. The furniture, like hers, was of antique style, and as in her house there were silver ornaments. There seemed to be Grandfather clocks everywhere, in the dining room, the sitting room and when she went up the stairs even on the landing. The whole effect, however, was charming. The piece de resistance, however, was a wonderful Jacobean dining room suite that Mr Garrow said had been inherited from his family. The garden was obviously designed, with ponds covered by a bridge. It was enchanting. The kitchen was neat, but perhaps needed a little modernising. It had two huge white cupboards.

Mr Garrow had a cabinet with wine and spirits. He made some sandwiches and Anne was able to have another Vodka and lime.

"You are continuing with your B. Ed," he said.

"Indeed," replied Anne, "but after getting home after school, there isn't a great deal of time to write essays or study."

"Why don't you stay here?" offered Mr Garrow. "You say that Robert has a flat and does not return in the week. This house is only 18 minutes from the school. You are very welcome to use the dining room as a study."

Anne was tempted. Like Robert, she did sometimes find the journey tedious, although it had almost become second nature to her. But the additional burden of studying after travelling was becoming hard. It was no use considering Robert because he certainly didn't consider her.

"I should have to return to Beaumont House at the weekend," she said.

"I understand that," conceded Mr Garrow. "But Monday to Friday, you would not have the burden of the journey."

"I think I will accept your offer," said Anne. "Thank you so much. Tuesday evenings of course I will be at College. I shall not return until after nine o'clock."

"Do whatever you wish," countered Mr Garrow. He then astounded her by saying, "Do you realise that I have fallen in love with you? I have admired you from the moment you came to the school. I know I made a stupid remark the other day, but in reality you have certainly achieved a lot at the school. The concerts that you have put together, the plays you have produced. The wonderful work you have done with the Recorder Group, and so much more. I admire you and I love you."

Anne felt like crying. Who had said this to her before? The only man in her life that loved her was her father. She didn't think Robert ever had. It was just a College friendship that turned into marriage, almost as a convenience. He had only been 22 when he married and hadn't had a chance to spread his wings.

Anne didn't really know how to answer.

"Please, call me Michael," he begged. "Mr Garrow is so formal for when we are away from school."

"I am honoured to hear what you say," said Anne. "But really I am now nearly asleep."

Michael showed her into a large bedroom with a large window overlooking the garden. The bed was made up. She was too tired to bath or shower. Staying in her underslip, she got into bed and slept.

The next morning Michael brought her tea and toast. She realised that her car was on his drive. What would the neighbours think? Michael was an Officer and a Gentleman, but her TR7 on his driveway would surely be noticed and people may draw a wrong conclusion.

However, she dressed and went to school as usual. She did not see Michael arrive at school. There was to be a staff meeting after school and Anne informed the staff of the excellence of the report and praised them of course for their contribution to its success.

After school Anne drove back to Beaumont House. She needed to leave money for the gardener, and collect some clothing. She also had to ring the contractor resurfacing her red driveway. It had not yet been completed. The cost was £350 and she agreed to send a cheque. The drive was to be completed the next day.

She once again drove to school. To her amazement, during the afternoon, the builder laying her drive appeared at her school demanding money.

"I have sent a cheque for £350," said Anne. "I posted it this morning."

"I underestimated how much tar macadam I would need. I need another £200." Anne had no choice but to give him another cheque. He had threatened to leave the drive unfinished. She couldn't have a scene at school.

She thought yet again, Robert had been to and from the house when convenient, but had contributed nothing. Thinking back, of all the bills she had paid for the house, it did make her feel bitter. She could not understand how Robert had never considered making any payment. There had been major problems such as a burst water tank requiring a ceiling repair, a leaking radiator, and so many more, but the worst of all was the six months absence when there was the fire and she really had struggled with money until the

Insurance money came through.

It hardened her resolve to stay with Michael Garrow. Apart from the weekends, this time it was she leaving Robert.

Chapter 48

Michael gave Anne a key and from Monday to Friday Anne let herself into the house. On Tuesdays of course she was late from college, but if there were no meetings at school, she let herself in, usually had a light snack such as coleslaw, then went into the dining room and studied or typed on her little Amstrad Computer. The room gradually became stacked with books ordered from the Open University, photocopies from books and microfiche. She usually researched these in-between the Tuesday lectures. Michael made no objection to his room turning into a library.

Anne did not look for him. They came back to the house separately, and as Anne was working, she had no idea what he ate. Sometimes she would break and they had a cup of tea together. They would reminisce over the day's events. Anne treasured these moments. The more time she spent in Michael's company, the more she appreciated his conduct as a gentleman and his intellect.

She had not known that his education at the City of London School was so excellent. He showed her his certificates from School Certificate to Additional Levels in Greek and Latin. He informed her of his Officer training from Sandhurst and told her that he had been twice mentioned in Despatches during World War II.

Robert knew now where she was and telephoned the school and said that he would pick her up on Saturdays at 10am. Anne had to go back to Beaumont House to clean the silver, dust the house, pick up post and give the garden some of her care. Robert did help in the garden. He was clearly not going to give up 'having a foot in the door'.

On Sunday evening Robert drove her back to Isleworth. Michael was wonderful. He always asked Robert inside, and had made a 'Hotpot' for them both. Anne felt that Robert did not really deserve such generous behaviour. Sometimes he seemed to outstay his welcome and Anne would cringe when he left, saying, "Thank you for the Hotpot. Lovely Hotpot, Michael." Anne presumed he went back to his flat. If he was living with someone, she wondered how he managed to escape at the weekends. Perhaps whoever it was, if there was someone, had a commitment at the weekend as well.

Anne had said to Robert, "Do you realise that I have virtually left you," but Robert seemed to ignore this! Once again the ostrich with its head in the sand.

There was a hiccup. Michael's divorce was final. As stated the two properties involved were of equal value, and Michael thought all was resolved. The ex-Mrs Garrow phoned Michael and said that she would like some of the items from the Isleworth house. All clothing and personal items of course had long since gone.

Michael was an Officer and a Gentleman. He had been married for many years, and felt guilty that he had not loved her. He did feel, however, that this had been mutual. He agreed that she could come to the house, to take any final things that she believed were hers. He did comment wryly that the Gloucestershire house was already full of antiques and artefacts and when he had last visited, now some time ago, it looked more like an antique shop.

Michael decided that he certainly wouldn't be at the house when she came. Anne of course could not be there either, although all her books were evidence itself that someone was there, plus some of her clothes in the wardrobe.

The visit was to be in the week. Michael booked them into a Plymouth Brethren Hotel (no alcohol) in Isleworth. The room had twin beds, but Anne now had no problem with being in the same room. They were booked in for two nights. The evening meal and breakfast were excellent, but they had to have a very hasty breakfast to get to school in time. This all worked well with no problems and the school day proceeded as usual.

They had obviously driven in their two cars to the hotel and on the third day drove back in the two cars to Isleworth. There was a shock. Michael's now ex-wife had taken so many things. The curtains had gone from the windows. The bedspreads had gone from the beds. A great deal of silver had gone. Even cutlery had gone from the drawers.

Michaels' face turned as if to stone. He was clearly very, very upset. Anne didn't know how to comfort him. He had been particularly fond of a gilt ormolu mantel clock and some Japanese figurines. Anne didn't know what to say but then said, "I will phone Robert and ask him to pick me up on Sunday morning instead of Saturday. We will go into Ealing where there is a large Department Store. We will purchase curtains and bedspreads."

Michael smiled. "A good idea. It is a bit of a shock. But I should have expected it. Her brother had a van and he must have accompanied her."

Anne didn't do any typing that evening, as she felt his sadness.

Anne thought ruefully that Robert had taken nothing from the Kenilworth house when he left, only his personal possessions, but he hadn't ever really left, had he?

The next day after school, Anne drove to a little antique shop that she had seen on the approach to Isleworth. The little shop was full of antiques and bric-a-brac. She bought some cutlery and some antique ornaments. She also purchased an ebony clock and some lovely flower vases (the vases, too, had gone).

When she returned to the house Michael was deeply moved. "How kind of you," he stated.

"You are being kind to me," replied Anne. Life is so much easier now with the short journey to and from school. It is also a very long way from Roehampton to Godalming. I am grateful to you."

CHAPTER 49

On Saturday they went to the Department Store and purchased ready-made curtains. They also purchased bedspreads. They had parked at the rear of the store and had to have help loading the items into the car. Michael had a large white estate car.

Anne had always had plenty of energy, so she hung the curtains and put the bedspreads onto the beds. Michael arranged the ornaments and sorted out the cutlery that was still left from the preceding evening. He loved the ebony clock. Normality seemed to reign again.

Anne could see that Michael was tired. He looked pale and drawn. They had had a snack in the store in Ealing, but Anne made some tea. There was bread and cheese so they had cheese on toast.

Anne looked at the garden. The lawn needed mowing. "Would you like me to mow the lawn?" she offered. "You must have a mower."

"Only a hand mower," stated Michael. Anne found it in an integral outside cupboard. Off she went, up and down and left the lawn in lovely stripes. It was a bit tricky because the lawn was shaped but she had had plenty of practice at Godalming and Kenilworth. After Robert had left, her father had mowed her lawn, but apart from that she had always mowed it, and it was a huge lawn with circular flower beds.

Strangely Jeremy had never once offered to mow her lawn, but then he didn't even mow his own.

Anne noticed that there were fish in the ponds. She loved that. She put the mower away, found the edging shears and went round the edge of the lawn. The neighbours must certainly have seen her activities, but she persevered. She even did some weeding. It was certainly quite a show garden and she had seen a similar one that had won a prize in the Daily Mail newspaper.

Michael was sitting in the living room and looked pale. She guessed that his asthma was playing up. He still, however, thanked her profusely and then drove to a little corner shop for provisions. They had soup for supper and went to bed.

Robert picked her up at 10 o'clock the next day. He said that he was having trouble with his eye and that it was like looking through the bottom of a milk bottle. He had been to a doctor, who recommended him to the Moorfields Eye Hospital in London. The doctor thought he had had a blood vessel burst in his eye as his blood pressure was high.

"Why couldn't I just have a nose bleed?" worried Robert. Robert was to have laser surgery on his eye the following week.

Anne did not let him do any gardening, but he still drove her back to Isleworth. "Do phone me and let me know how you get on," Anne asked Robert. She could see that he was very worried. Sight is very precious.

Michael had been to the shops again. All the small shops now seemed to be open on Sundays, and 'Hotpot' was on the menu. Michael was decent enough to be concerned about Robert's eye.

Robert phoned her at school on Wednesday. "The doctor has contacted me," he said. "They want to get my blood pressure down before I go to Moorfields for laser surgery. I am going into St Bartholomew's Hospital today for observation. I feel frightened. Can you come and see me?"

Anne did not hesitate. "I will come this evening," she said.

Anne told Michael where she was going after school. She drove to his house and left the car on the drive. Anne walked to Osterley Tube Station. She hadn't a clue where Barts Hospital was, but knew that it was located somewhere in the City of London. The nearest tube station was St Paul's. The tube train time was over half an hour, 37 minutes to be exact. Anne then had to find the hospital which she did by asking, and then had to find the ward in which Robert was ensconced. He was in his pyjamas, looking very pathetic.

"I am not sure how long I shall be in here," he stated. "I just want my eye fixed."

Anne knew that Robert's father had had some blood pressure and heart problems and thought that it was probably inherited. As she stood by Robert's bed, a girl walked in. She totally ignored Anne. She was of medium height, probably younger than Robert, but with scruffy tousled ginger hair. She began to talk to Robert, and they had a conversation in which Anne could not possibly join in. Robert was speaking to this girl enthusiastically. There were no introductions. Robert was totally ignoring her. Anne had managed to arrive at Barts for 6.30pm and had expected to stay until about 8 o'clock. However, Robert only had eyes for his new visitor. No name was given and they both continued to totally ignore Anne. Anne spent the time chatting to a man in the next bed, who had no visitor. At 8 o'clock the girl turned to leave. Robert said an enthusiastic "Goodbye" to her. Both women went to the lift to go down. The girl did not speak and just left as the doors opened.

Anne had to make the journey back. She guessed that this girl must be somehow involved with the flat that Robert was now occupying. They appeared too familiar to be work colleagues. They seemed to have so much to talk about.

When Robert asked for her to visit him, he had obviously not realised that this unnamed girl would also immediately visit. He must have told her where he was, however. As usual, Robert's life was a mystery. No wonder he wanted another flat.

Anne got back to Isleworth feeling very dejected. She certainly didn't plan to visit Robert again. She told Michael of the events at the hospital. "I think he may be in there for a week," she guessed.

"I think we should go on a break for the weekend," suggested Michael. "Let me take you to Lulworth Cove."

"I went camping near there," stated Anne, "at Durdle Door with Jeremy and the boys." She had told him about that stage of her life, of course. "We did visit Lulworth Cove. It is indeed a beauty spot."

"I will book a hotel tomorrow," promised Michael. "Leave Robert to his ginger-haired girlfriend. It will not hurt to leave your house in Godalming."

Anne accepted gratefully. She felt so hurt and humiliated with Robert's treatment. She had responded immediately to his cri de coeur, and again he had let her down. Even if he was living with this girl in the flat (perhaps she was not there at weekends!), surely he could have had the good manners to introduce them to each other. She guessed the girl knew who she was because of the total refusal to acknowledge her in any way. Anne did telephone the hospital and Robert was still under observation. They stated that he would probably be discharged on Monday.

Chapter 50

Michael drove Anne to Lulworth. He was a good consensus considerate driver. Robert, used to London traffic, always drove rather too fast for Anne's peace of mind. The hotel that Michael had found was situated with a sea view. It was only a short walk to the cove. There was one bedroom with one double bed. Anne was not surprised at this. Their relationship had moved forward and she felt at peace with Michael. They had so many similar interests, their love of antiques, and their love of classical music. Michael always had classical music playing in his car. If anything, he had had a better background than she. Her father had been a Police Officer, his father had been a Headmaster, but had married into a wealthy family. Even his mother had been to university, almost unheard of for women in those days. He had had a nanny as a child and attended a private school. She had passed the scholarship to a Grammar School. He had been to Sandhurst, and passed out as an Officer.

She considered the men in her life. Her father she loved dearly, she was an only daughter and much loved by him. Jeremy had made her feel like a woman as opposed to Robert who made her feel like his mother. She felt that he was like a recalcitrant child. When she was away from school, with Michael, he made her feel like a lady.

The food at the hotel was excellent, although she had not expected the consommé soup to be cold. They went to bed and for the first time Michael made love to her. It just seemed a natural evolution after all that had gone on before.

Robert had re-enforced the fact by deed and action that he had no real caring for her at all. Jeremy was now married and she hoped happy. She had heard from his son Anthony who had kept in touch strangely, who said that his father and Charmaine had moved to Lockerbie in Scotland. They had bought a cottage. Jeremy had wanted to live in the Lake District, but property was too expensive. Jeremy had finished building his boat, however, and had sailed it on Lake Windermere.

Anne was very happy in Michael's company. They explored Lulworth Cove the next day. Anne tried to do some rock climbing, but it defeated her. She became frightened and climbed down.

Soon it was time for the return journey, but their relationship had moved to a new level.

When they returned to Isleworth Anne no longer went into the second bedroom. She snuggled in with Michael and felt that all was well with the world.

At school, they were careful to maintain a very professional relationship. They behaved just as they had when Anne first entered the school as Headteacher. She referred to him, of course, as Mr Garrow, and he to her as Mrs Deighton.

Robert did phone her in the week and said that he was having the laser surgery on Wednesday. It was an outpatients procedure. Anne wished him well. He said that he would again pick her up on Saturday.

When they got back to Godalming, Anne asked about the girl at the hospital. Robert admitted that it was actually her flat that he was in, but of course he was contributing rent. He said that she also worked for ICL, but liaised between England and Germany, working on the technical side of computer science. He admitted that he had driven with her to the Hague in the Netherlands for a Conference. About his eye, he said that they were unable to clear it in one session and that he would have to attend again.

Robert did some shopping for food and Anne again attended to post, dusted the house and did some gardening.

CHAPTER 51

Michael made no objection to her being with Robert in her house at the weekend. Anne thought he realised that if a divorce was going to occur, it would have already done so. Of course, in fact, it nearly did. He realised that Anne really did believe the words she had uttered in Church 'For better or worse'. It was her mother that had in fact contacted the divorce lawyer when Robert first left. Anne also felt that it was admission of failure, but that had been re-enforced so many times it was ludicrous.

Robert drove Anne back to Michael's and Michael had prepared a Hotpot, and Robert said, "Hotpot, Hotpot, Lovely Hotpot!" Anne wondered if the ginger girl gave him Hotpot at the flat. Robert said that he had a business meeting the next weekend. Anne wondered if it was in the Hague, Hamburg, Berlin or Dresden maybe.

When she told Michael, he suggested that they went away again. She had been working on her degree on Tuesday as before and typing each night until nearly midnight. She was well in advance as this was a year-long course. She felt that she could spare the time and agreed.

They drove to a lovely hotel in Hampshire. It was once probably an Old Manor House. Anne had lost all sense of direction because they seemed to drive over old cattle grids onto unknown countryside. However, when she saw the hotel, it was well worth the journey. The rooms were large and spacious, and their bedroom overlooked lawns edged with topiary. There was even a knot garden, so called because the plants were planted in a pattern resembling a knot. (The design of the knot garden was adapted from one of four laid out by the Rev. Walter Stonehouse between 1631 and 1640.)

Once again, the food was excellent, and again they shared a double bed. Michael's love making was not as exhilarating as that of Jeremy, nor as physically satisfying, but he was an older man and Anne was contented to feel loved and cared for.

It was a lovely experience to be in such a grand old house that had been adapted into a hotel. They travelled back to Isleworth on the Sunday.

The same pattern continued. Anne going to college on Tuesdays and typing her notes and essays in the evening after school.

Anne wanted to change her car. The TR7 was going out of production and there was no replacement. The factory in Coventry was closing. The nearest replacement was a Fiat X19, a rather smart sports car. Michael's car was very old, and he offered to buy her TR7 at trade price. Anne accepted this and ordered the Fiat X19. When it arrived at a garage in Whitton, Anne was delighted. It had a vermillion red bonnet and boot with a black roof and doors. It looked outstanding. Anne drove back to Isleworth full of delight.

She drove the car to school in the ensuing days and also to a local Comprehensive School, where she was sometimes invited for lunches with Councillors. The local comprehensive schools all wished for the children from her school to progress to their school. The reason was that her school was in a good catchment area with well behaved children, supportive parents and also due to the excellent reputation of her school.

However, one morning she went to get into her car as usual. There were multitudinous scratches over the doors on one side. Anne initially thought this may have occurred in the car park at her school. She could not believe that any of her children had done this, and her office window overlooked the car park. She wondered, however, if she just had not noticed it when driving home in the evening twilight.

When at school she was not claiming on her Insurance and asked the same garage to respray the damage. During this time Michael did have to drive her to and from school, but despite their precautions most of the staff had realised their friendship. Even one councillor had stated that he had heard that she studied at Mr Garrow's house. This was of course true.

It was an expensive respray but Anne had to bear the cost. The garage returned the car to her school.

Anne visited the local Comprehensive School again. They were due for their Ofsted Inspection and wished for her recorder group to play during their Assembly and for her choir to accompany their choir in "Joseph and his Amazing Technicolour Dreamcoat," words by Tim Rice and music by Andrew Lloyd Webber.

The next morning as she climbed into her car, she again noticed numerous scratchers all over the doors on one side of the car. Her heart sank. How was this happening? She telephoned the Headmaster, Mr Goddard, at the Comprehensive School she had visited. She explained that there were scratches on her car and wondered if it could have occurred in his school car park. He was not offended, but stated that he had prefects on duty in the car park during the lunch hour and also a Senior Member of Staff, as during this time there were usually several visitors requiring parking space. It was of course during her lunch hour that Anne had visited and indeed she had been directed to a parking space by a school prefect.

Anne apologised for inconveniencing him but explained that this was the second time that it had happened and that she was concerned.

Again, the car was resprayed and returned to her. Then again the scratches occurred. Anne contacted the Police. She felt that this was not being done at either school, but by somebody in the neighbourhood.

The police car was outside the house and the officer was extremely helpful. By chance, one of the neighbours was in the house when the officer arrived. He had come to ask Michael if he could borrow his tree topper. He heard the initial discussion before the officer left. The officer felt that it was someone in the neighbourhood. Maybe someone who went to work on an early shift and was performing the vandalism maybe in the very early morning. The officer felt that it was significant that the violation was always on one side, the same side of the car that was facing away from the house windows. The officer promised to provide a police presence in the early hours after the car was once more resprayed.

The car was never again scratched. Anne could only assume that someone very much resented her living at Mr Garrow's house.

CHAPTER 52

A nother catastrophe occurred. Very sadly Robert's father died. He had had heart problems for several years. Robert himself was now well. He was taking tablets to help his blood pressure and the laser surgery had restored his vision.

When Robert picked her up on the Saturday, he asked if she would attend his father's funeral. She of course agreed. Robert organised the funeral, but of course his mother paid for it.

There was an embarrassing moment when one relation came to Anne and said, "Who are you?" Anne replied curtly, "Robert's wife." She had been allowed time from school but did not stay long. What did concern her was that Robert was laughing and joking at the ensuing wake at the house and appeared totally unfazed by his father's death.

Robert announced to her the next weekend that he was going on a sailing holiday with a Tony Laurence. This guy apparently made up exhibition stands for the sale of computers. Robert had been able to give him work. This trip was a type of bonus. They were going to sail around the north of France in a 44' boat owned by Laurence. Anne thought that he was very fortunate to receive this offer.

During this time, she, as usual, carried on with her studies at Michael's house and returned to Beaumont House at the weekend. Michael never asked to, or stayed at Beaumont House.

When Anne eventually saw Robert again, he talked enthusiastically about the trip. Anne felt sorry for Robert's mother now on her own. She was only 70, but seemed to be giving up on life according to Robert. Because of his lifestyle, he had only visited her twice since his father's funeral. Anne suggested that he invite her to Beaumont House for the weekend.

Anne explained the situation to Michael as she said that she would be driving from Godalming to school on the Monday.

Robert had had a new firm's car now for some time, so Anne thought that at least at work he must be doing well. It was a Passat estate. Plus the 'bribe' of his trip round the north of France; he seemed to be doing very well.

Robert brought his mother to the house. She was low in spirits, but had always been a rather neurotic woman. She told them that now she rarely left the house. A neighbour did her shopping and fetched her pension. Another friend fetched her library books.

At lunch on the Saturday and Sunday, Robert's mother wanted to know all about his sailing trip. Robert spent a long time talking about this, the boat, the places they visited and the weather. Apparently, Tony Laurence had a chef and an assistant on board who provided all the meals. It certainly sounded a wonderful trip.

Robert took his mother home but did not return. Anne did no studying. She cleaned up and washed the bed linen and then ironed it.

Robert had changed his jacket when he took his mother home. He had always kept some clothes at the house. For some reason he had arrived in a blazer and had changed into a suit from the wardrobe. He had left his blazer lying on the bed. Anne idly picked it up and was going to hang it up. A piece of paper was poking from the top pocket and inquisitively she pulled it out. It was a docket from ICL giving Robert permission to take the Passat car to Belgium and Germany on exactly the dates that he said he had been sailing.

Anne realised at once that the whole story of sailing around the north of France with Tony Laurence was a complete fabrication. He had obviously taken someone to Belgium and Germany, probably 'ginger hair' and had invented the whole trip.

What bothered Anne the most was the fact that he had spent a considerable amount of time telling his mother about the trip. Several hours in fact. The places visited, the hospitality and the food. She couldn't understand why he hadn't just said he was going to a conference or to a launch. The worse thing was lying to his mother. She began to think that Robert was becoming a Walter Mitty and a complete fantasist.

It upset her greatly. She was a logical creature and could not understand why he had invented this quid pro quo, a sailing trip for favours, when it was so untrue and seemed totally unnecessary. She felt that Robert had done so many strange things she should not really be surprised, but she still searched for a logical reason and could find none. When she did next see Robert, she of course mentioned the ICL permission to take the car abroad and he could not deny the evidence. He admitted that the whole story was an invention, but just said it was a stupid thing to have said. He admitted that he had accompanied 'ginger hair' – whose name seemed to change from Valerie one minute and Barbara the next – to the Hague. He said that she had then gone to Germany to a meeting on her own. Anne decided that she certainly was not going to hear the truth of this at all.

Robert then told her that he was getting short of money. He said that he could no longer really afford rent at the flat.

Anne had to second guess this. Was Barbara or Valerie giving up her flat? Why was Robert short of money? As said before, he gave her no money whatsoever. He still paid nothing towards the expenses of Beaumont House, not even council tax.

"I suppose you could stay here in the week," Anne volunteered. "But I shall continue to stay at Isleworth. All my books and research papers are there and I prefer the short journey to school."

"Well, I may carry on for a bit at the flat," Robert said. "I haven't really thought it through. I don't like the long journey either."

CHAPTER 53

L ife continued. Anne was now in the second year of her degree and was working hard each evening at Isleworth. Robert still picked her up on Saturdays and took her back on Sundays for Hotpot! This continued for some time. She had some examinations and once again was given time from school for study.

The adjoining house in Isleworth was having double glazing installed. Bang! Bang! Bang! She could not concentrate. When Michael came home from school, she said she just couldn't study with all the daily noise. She would drive to Godalming and study there. It was only for a week. She took the books she actually needed (as hinted by Dr Jefferson, her tutor), and drove home.

Lovely! Peace and quiet. She had obviously picked up some groceries for food. But when she walked in there was another surprise. The kitchen was messy and the bed unmade. She was reminded of 'Goldilocks and the Three Bears' – "Who's been sleeping in my bed?"

She left it all and went to the bedroom upstairs and studied her books. At 7 o'clock the front door opened and in walked Robert. He looked aghast when he saw her.

"What are you doing here?" he stuttered.

"Actually, this is my home. What are you doing here?" replied Anne.

Robert owned up. "I have been living here for some time. The flat in Wandsworth has gone. Rents are now exorbitant."

"But you picked me up on Saturday, and when I came in everything was as I left it. Even the post was left by the letterbox."

"I tidied up. I didn't want you to know that I was living here. I travelled up on Saturday to fetch you and returned here on Sunday night."

"But why?" queried Anne. "I said you could stay here. It was so deceitful leaving the post on the floor. Why oh why do you do it?"

Robert had no answer. He could in fact have gone to his mother's house in Carshalton. That would certainly have been nearer to work, but he may then have been obliged to do more for her, and this would not suit him. Anne felt betrayed once again by his deceit. She also realised that once again he would be living in Godalming.

Anne returned to Isleworth and sat the examinations at Roehampton. If she passed she would be able to add B.Ed. after her name, but she was determined to continue to obtain the Honours.

CHAPTER 54

A nne was not 'in love' with Michael, but she loved him. His kindness to her was outstanding.

Many years earlier she had had a high temperature and had to wait to see a doctor. Robert had been with Jessica at the time. He had come in at 2.30 in the morning and just said, "How are you?" She had been in bed ill all day on her own. She did go to the doctors on the following day and got amoxicillin which cured her almost immediately.

She had been at the Hounslow School one day taking a netball group. She had felt so ill. From the welfare cabinet she took a thermometer and took her temperature. It was 103 degrees. When she got back to Isleworth, Michael had insisted on taking her to A&E, where she again received antibiotics. The contrast to Robert's behaviour was immense.

Another time she cut her thumb badly on the edge of a corned beef tin. Again, Michael had taken her to A&E for it to be dressed.

If she went to the hairdressers in Hounslow, and it was raining, he would meet her with an umbrella. She was humbled by his kindness. He had even been meeting her from college in recent times and riding shotgun behind her on the way home.

She repaid him in some small way in kind. She bought him some gilt-edged mirrors for the house and a lovely oval Regency coffee table for the sitting room. She also bought some double sheepskin rugs. It was so wonderful to feel cared for as opposed to Robert's ever present cavalier attitude. He only ever considered what was most suitable for himself.

Anne began her additional Honours Degree Course. Michael was unhappy about this, which was not surprising. She spent hours in his dining room typing and studying. The only respite was when there were late meetings at the school. Anne still went back to Godalming on Saturday and Robert still collected her and brought her back for Hotpot. Robert did do some interior decorating whilst at the house, and even paid for the paint and emulsion.

At Christmas, Robert went to his mother. Anne decided to introduce Michael to her parents. They were happy for her to spend Christmas Day with them. Michael drove down the M1 to Northampton and then to Wellingborough.

Anne had obviously told her parents about Michael on the telephone. They were delighted that she was with such a caring gentleman.

The visit went very well and Anne's mother asked his shoe size, and promised to send him a pair of Barkers shoes, for which she had the franchise.

On the way back there was a tyre problem. Anne was very concerned, but Michael was able to change the wheel. She was impressed with this – not only an Officer and a Gentleman, but a car mechanic as well!

CHAPTER 55

Anne was going to take a party of school children skiing. This was a first for this age group in Hounslow. She had had to propose the advantages to the children at an Education Meeting. The proposed ski trip was to be in Sauze d'Oulx in Italy. They were going in the half term. Michael of course was now not fit enough to ski although once he had been excellent at sports such as rugby. His asthma had developed much later in life resulting from his war wound, but despite this he had been a member of the Twickenham Rugby Club and was now Vice President.

Again, Anne was short on adult help. Two members of staff volunteered, but once again Anne asked Robert. This time he was very keen indeed. He had missed out years ago and happily agreed.

The children left by road from the school to Heathrow Airport. The hotel to which they transferred was again excellent and once again as at her previous school, these children were fitted out with boots, skis and poles. They had ski lessons as had her children in Richmond. They all learned to snow plough and quickly learned how to manage the ski lifts. Robert had studied his ski books and seemed quickly to be able to do parallel skiing. He was put into the 'gold' class. Everyone else was in silver, including Anne. They all gained their silver medals. This trip was a great success although one child insisted on buying toy cars with his pocket money when they visited the village. After the trip the boy's father came to the school and complained to Anne about the number of toy cars his son had bought. However, a week later he returned and said that his son had had such a wonderful time and that he could talk of nothing else. The father thanked Anne profusely for giving his son the opportunity to be so happy and to learn to ski.

The time went on, school life as usual, school sports, school plays, concerts, school life. Anne continued with the Honours degree and Robert did not get another flat (to her knowledge!).

Anne did find a Christmas card that he had discarded, however.

"I can't wait to see you again. Love Pauline."

Leopards do not change their spots, Anne thought ruefully.

Anne guessed that Barbara or Valerie had vanished from the scene and now there was a Pauline. He was clearly not living with Pauline, however, and Anne made a guess that she had a partner or was married.

Anne again had study leave and again took her examinations.

It was time for Michael's retirement. Anne was putting together a concert of songs from the World War II era. She changed some words to incorporate his name. But then another sad event took place.

Robert stated that his mother was suffering badly from constipation. Anne suggested a laxative such as senokot and a visit to her doctor. Robert reported that she resisted these suggestions. Robert phoned her at school and said that his mother had fallen ill. She had asked a neighbour for help and had been taken to St Helier Hospital.

After school, Anne immediately drove to the hospital. The hospital had already taken Robert's mother into theatre, but her intestine had ruptured and sadly she died. Robert was absolutely devastated. He wept bitterly and Anne was full of pity. Anne knew that Robert did not want to go back to his mother's house at this moment. She knew to whom she could turn. She suggested that Robert drove back with her to Isleworth. As usual Michael was there like a rock. He understood the situation and made tea for Robert who was stunned. He made a meal and was compassionate. He allowed Robert to stay the night. Anne had known that she could totally rely upon him. Robert was able to return to Carshalton the next morning when he made all necessary arrangements.

Anne and Michael returned to school as usual. Anne felt so grateful to Michael, that even though he had heard and knew of Robert's shortcomings, he had shown compassion. Just like the Good Samaritan in the Bible.

Robert's mother's funeral happened to have been arranged in Anne's half term holiday. Michael understood that Anne needed to attend and to help. Robert drove Anne to Carshalton in his firm's Passat. Anne had not been into the house for years. After her very lukewarm reception on the night of the fire at Beaumont House, she had never wished to return. In any case, due to circumstances, she had not deemed it either suitable, nor had it been possible.

As she stepped out of Robert's car, she could see at once that the front garden was neglected. When she entered the front door to the house she was dismayed. The rooms were dusty and uncared for. She had never before encountered such dust. It lay in balls of grey fluff on the surface of shelves and bookcases. The kitchen walls were deplorable. Huge vertical streaks of dirt were on the walls.

Robert's mother had once been very house proud. Her furniture may have been very 1930s, but it was spotlessly clean. When Anne had first entered the house as Robert's girlfriend at the age of 19, as previously stated, it did not have the antique furniture and valuable ornaments that were in her parents' home, but it had been immaculate. Robert's mother had clearly lost interest in her home after her husband's death, and when she had become unwell she obviously became unable to look after the house. Robert had clearly done nothing to help his mother. He could easily have driven from Putney to his mother's house and either helped to clean it himself or employed a cleaner to do so.

Anne went into the rear garden. The lawn was now full of weeds, as were the flower beds. Robert's father had once loved his garden. The lawns were once manicured and the flower beds well tended. Obviously no gardener had been deployed and Robert must seldom have bothered to mow the lawn if he did visit.

Anne was quite shocked. She had taken clothes with her including a suit and hat for the funeral, of course, but she did not have a great deal of clothing with her. She took off her dress and found an old smock belonging to her mother-in-law. She ordered Robert to find the garden mower and to try to improve and mow the lawns. She knew that it was impossible to remove all the weeds from the flower beds.

She herself got a bowl of hot water and detergent and tried to remove the black streaks of grime from the kitchen walls. Despite several attempts at this, she knew that she would have to try again the next day. The dirt was so embedded.

She found the vacuum cleaner from a room underneath the stairs and proceeded to vacuum the floors. She used the vacuum tools to suck the fluff, where possible, from various surfaces. Where this was not possible, she used a damp cloth and a duster.

The house began to look a little better. Fortunately, the bed they had once slept in many years ago, still had bed linen on it. It smelt musty but Anne could not worry about that. There was too much still to be done in too short a time. The wake was to be at this house in two days' time and the next day Robert had to collect his Aunt Doris from her home. She was going to assist with organising refreshments after they had been purchased.

They slept in the musty, dusty bed. Robert had purchased some groceries before collecting her from Isleworth, so, before they went to bed they were able to partake of some food and drink.

The next day Robert left to pick up his Aunt Doris (his mother's sister), and Anne provided him with a list of items they would need for the wake following the funeral. It would appear that at least 30 family and friends were to attend.

Anne spent more time cleaning and dusting and spent even more time working on the kitchen walls. Later on, the kitchen itself. It had been modernised through the efforts of Robert's father, but now looked neglected.

Aunt Doris came and Anne set out the dining room table for preparation for the plates of food they had started to prepare in the kitchen. All cups and glasses had to be washed as there was no dishwasher. It all took a long time and they were busy all day. Anne had had no communication with Michael. She did not ring because she knew that it was not necessary. They now had such an affinity that she knew he would realise there was much to be done in the normal preparation for a funeral. He would have no comprehension of the situation she had walked into, of course.

Funerals are dreadful. Robert was certainly not laughing at his mother's as he had at his father's funeral. Anne and Aunt Doris had prepared the refreshments well.

Some unpleasant incidents occurred. A Mrs MacGill (a friend of Robert's mother) appeared to look very self-important. She seemed to sit smugly in a chair, listening to the other guests who mainly seemed to be praising Robert's father to the detriment of the poor lady whose funeral they had just attended.

In a quiet moment, Mrs MacGill asked Robert if she could have returned a little coronation coach she said she had lent many years ago. Robert was not sure where this was and promised to find it and return it to her the next day. Other cousins were helping to clear up in the kitchen and were arguing about the value of the 1930s cups and saucers. One cousin, Noel, commented that the cooker had seen better days.

Anne wondered if they were expecting some largesse. She herself had no interest in anything in the house and had already suggested that it would no doubt be his mother's wish for her sister, Aunt Doris, to inherit her jewellery and furs. Robert had agreed to this as he had heard this previously mentioned by his mother.

At last the mourners departed. Robert had to drive Aunt Doris to her home. He had told Doris that he would collect her again in the near future to sort out his mother's possessions.

Anne cleared away the remaining discarded empty tea cups, wine glasses and leftover food. She ensured that the house was left as neat and clean as possible. Robert returned and she spent what was to be her last night ever in the Carshalton house.

The next morning they were leaving. Before taking Anne back to Isleworth, Robert had found the little coronation coach which to his belief had been around in his home for many years. He took it to the MacGills. Anne waited in the car. He returned white faced.

Apparently as soon as he had reached the door it opened, and Mr MacGill took the coach, but said, "Did your mother make a will? She promised us £1000."

"I am afraid my mother did not make a will," he stated. As an only son, he would inherit.

Mr MacGill shouted to his wife. "She didn't leave a will. She hasn't left us the money."

Robert was so disgusted he just walked away.

When Anne heard of this episode, she realised why Mrs MacGill was looking so complacent at the funeral. She was happily expecting a legacy of £1000.

Robert knew that as there was no will (his mother would never have had the courage or inclination to consult with a solicitor), a solicitor would have to be consulted for probate. He said to Anne that after he had taken her to Isleworth, he would attend to this.

Michael once again welcomed Robert kindly before he departed to the solicitor's office. Robert would then have to go into work. It was Anne's half term holiday, but Robert had to have been granted compassionate leave of absence.

Anne returned to Godalming on the Saturday. Robert arranged for probate to be set in motion and to take Aunt Doris to the house the following Monday. He had arranged for the personal items belonging to his mother, that Aunt Doris did not wish for, to be collected by a charity shop. He said that after Monday, he would lock up the house and for the present it would be just left unattended.

Anne was still busy at school planning for Michael's retirement. Children, parents and staff were making a collection for his retirement. Michael did state, to Anne's surprise, that he did not wish anyone to choose his retirement gifts. He wished to choose them himself. He maybe thought that this was his due through the time he had spent at the school. Quite a large sum of money was raised.

The concert for Michael went well and parents were even standing at the rear of the hall as there were no further chairs available. He thanked the choir for their rendition of some of his favourite songs.

The actual leaving ceremony was very poignant. Staff and the PTA organised all the refreshments and he received many gifts including a gardening book, a cut glass decanter, an antique bowl, a magnifying glass, to name but a few. The items he had chosen from the collection were an antique set of drawers and a set of glasses inscribed with the school's crest of a stag's head.

Of course, a new Deputy Head had had to be appointed. The interviews had taken place in the school library and an appointment had been made. Anne tried to keep this in low profile, because she knew that Michael would greatly miss the school.

CHAPTER 56

Amazingly enough, Michael had suggested that they go on holiday to Egypt, where he had once served on the Officer Selection Panel during World War II after he had been wounded.

He himself suggested that Robert accompany them. He meant this kindly as he knew that Robert was suffering from the loss of his mother. They booked up for a river cruise on the Nile. They went immediately after the school broke up for the summer holiday. Anne had learned that she now certainly had been awarded her Honours Degree and could put B.Ed (Hons) (London) after her name.

At least for the time being she need not study, but she resolved to continue with a Masters Degree. Michael was upset about this. He knew that Anne had 14 more years as Head, but he had hoped there would be company for himself in the evenings. He realised there would be even more research needed and a whole dissertation to be written. He felt that the future looked bleak. To prevent days being too empty, Anne was able to arrange some part-time teaching for him at the school. She hoped that this would give him a continued link with the school that he loved.

Anne loved Egypt. The boat was luxurious, and stopped at all the temples. Anne stayed with Robert in one cabin and Michael was in a cabin nearby. Michael accepted this because he knew that Robert had no sexual interest in Anne whatsoever, but they were still married.

They disembarked from the boat at Luxor and travelled by coach to the Abu Simbel. Robert began to feel very ill. On the journey he became delirious and he had to have some medical attention. They returned by coach to Luxor and by now several members of the party were being violently sick. At Luxor they were taken by train to Cairo. The facilities on the train were appalling. Most people who were on the same trip became ill. Michael was fine, but even Anne became sick.

In Cairo they visited the Great Pyramids of Giza and of course the Sphinx. Michael enjoyed seeing these monuments once again. Robert still felt unwell but rallied a little.

It was soon time to return home. They flew from Cairo to Heathrow where they picked up their cars. Michael returned to Isleworth and Anne and Robert to Godalming.

Anne and Robert still felt slightly nauseous, but Michael after being at Isleworth for a few days developed a high fever. He phoned to say that he had to go to hospital.

Robert returned to work (but was still feeling below par). Anne continued to feel slightly nauseous, but it occurred in waves. Anne of course drove to Isleworth and visited Michael in hospital. She was concerned and apprehensive. He seemed in good spirits. She kept his house clean and looked after the garden. The doctors soon found the cause of Michael's fever. It was Guardia Lambia, a flagellated unicellular eukaryotic micro-organism which caused an infection in the small intestine. The doctors gave Michael Metronidazole Flagyl and he was soon discharged and allowed to return home. Anne was so overjoyed to see him as she had been so very worried when he was in hospital. She had ensured that the house and garden looked perfect.

Anne and Robert both obtained Metronidazole from their doctor in Godalming as they realised that this was also the cause of Robert's illness and Anne's nausea. Despite their brush with Guardia Lambia (no doubt ingested from drinking water and vegetables washed in water such as lettuce, and ice could also have caused the problem), they all had very much enjoyed the experience of Egypt and Michael had loved to return there.

The school term started again. Anne registered at Roehampton for her Masters Degree and Michael came to the school for four days of the week. The new Deputy Head, Mr Sydney, seemed to develop a very good relationship with the staff and he was an excellent teacher. He had had several articles on wildlife published in magazines.

One thing Anne had not foreseen. The impact of Michael being in the school with another person as Deputy Head. She had even forgotten about Michael's lunch. As Deputy Head, the cook in the school canteen had always taken his school meal into the staffroom for him on a tray, where he had always eaten it at a corner table. Anne did not realise this was no longer happening as he made no complaint. It was not until the School Secretary asked if she realised this was no longer happening, that Anne realised her folly. Not only was he feeling unimportant but was feeling more sidelined with the prerogative of his school lunch taken away. At once she asked the cook to rectify this and offered, if necessary, to pay for the meal. She had been so busy with her recorder groups that she was totally unaware of the distress this must have caused him.

Michael began to suffer from asthmatic attacks more frequently. Anne was unaware how serious these could be and felt that they were mainly psychological. Michael did tell her that he had confided in a neighbour that maybe it was a mistake to have undertaken the part-time teaching at the school where he no longer had the authority and prestige of being the Deputy Head.

Anne continued her Tuesday sessions at Roehampton, but it was now more intense. Much more research was needed and students were expected to give lectures themselves, which involved more preparation. Anne was unable to spend a great deal of time now with Michael.

One morning when she was going to school, on the same day that he was to attend, he had a bad asthma attack. He had his ventolin inhaler and said he would be alright. Anne left for school but did worry until he arrived. She did not realise, however, how this attack foretold the impending tragedy.

CHAPTER 57

One Friday night they had had a cuddle in the sitting room. Anne was so tired after her day at school that she actually went to bed with her pullover on. When she awoke Michael was sitting on the edge of the bed. "I don't feel well," he said. "Can you make me a cup of tea?"

Anne got up immediately. As she did so, Michael began to gasp, "Oh God! Oh God!" Anne forgot about the tea and dialled 999. As she was talking to the operator she could hear Michael still saying, "Oh God! Oh God!" She asked the operator to send for an ambulance immediately. She rushed back upstairs. Michael had his ventolin inhaler in his hand. She put her arm around him and took the inhaler. She put it to his mouth. "Breathe this in," she urged. As she said this he just collapsed on the landing floor. There was a doctor in a nearby house and she rushed there for help. She was told he was on a call. The paramedics arrived. They put Michael in a type of chair and carried him down the stairs to the ambulance.

She heard one of them say, "Has he gone?" The other paramedic said, "I think so."

Anne couldn't grasp this. She thought that Michael had fainted. Another neighbour who was a nurse saw the ambulance and came in. Anne and the neighbour drove to the West Middlesex Hospital to which Michael had been taken. Anne was distraught. They waited in a waiting room and a doctor came to say that they had managed to get Michael's heart beating again. Anne had not understood that it had stopped. They advised her to go home, as nothing could be done at that moment. She and the neighbour returned to Isleworth. Anne thanked the neighbour for her concern.

It was still early on Saturday morning and not yet time for Robert to pick her up. She phoned him and said that Michael was in hospital. He said he would drive up immediately.

When he arrived, they returned to the hospital. Michael was unconscious and the doctors said they would do some tests, but they were afraid that he was brain dead. He was alive, however, so Anne still had hope.

Robert stayed with her at Isleworth. Anne did some typing but they returned again to the hospital. There was no change.

Robert had to go to work on Monday and Anne went to school. She wept as she told the staff of the situation. Luckily it was an Inset Day with a speaker. Anne explained her situation to the speaker and Mr Sydney, the Deputy Head, organised the day. Anne was distraught in her office. She returned to the hospital and held Michael's hand. He was totally unresponsive. She had taken his favourite pocket watch for him to hold but of course he could not. She still went to College on Tuesday, but was weeping so much, a female lecturer was sent to comfort her. She only went to College because she did not know what to do with herself. She of course could not attend any lectures. She drove back to the hospital. Two other members of staff were now there as well. Michael was still totally unresponsive and a doctor told her that sadly he was indeed brain dead. He was on a ventilator but there was little purpose in continuing.

Anne could see Michael though a glass pane. She suddenly saw doctors pumping on his chest. They stopped. They came in to her. The two female members of staff were also there and told them that he had died. The doctors said they had attempted resuscitation to no avail.

Anne couldn't think. One member of staff suggested that she leave her car at the hospital, and kindly drove her back to Isleworth. The other member of staff followed. Robert came in from work; he obviously had realised the gravity of the situation. The nurse who had tried to help knocked at the door to inquire about the situation, and came in.

It was all in slow motion. Anne just sat there totally stunned, shocked and full of grief. Only two men had loved her in her life, her father and Michael, and now one of them had gone.

Anne castigated herself time and time again, for not realising that Michael's heart had just stopped when he collapsed in the house. He had suffered so long with asthma and the ventolin inhaler had always eased the symptoms. She asked herself over and over again why had she not tried resuscitation or massaged his heart instead of rushing to find a doctor. She had not realised that he had actually died at that moment. She had, however, become almost paralysed with worry and thought a doctor could better assist.

The doctors at the hospital told her that there was little she could have done. Michael's bronchial tubes were too inflamed and filled with mucus. They had restarted his heart with mechanical support, but brain death was irreversible.

Anne still played the situation over and over again in her mind. She should have realised how deeply traumatic it was for Michael to no longer be a full-time member of the school that he loved.

Anne of course had to organise Michael's funeral. Hounslow Council granted permission for the school to close early in order that staff may attend.

Anne had some previously prescribed Diazepam and took four tablets. She could not demean herself publicly with her grief.

The crematorium was filled with people wishing to pay their last respects to a dedicated teacher. Many staff returned to the home at Isleworth for the wake. The catering had been organised for her by the Welfare Assistant at the school. The diazepam made Anne almost totally unaware of events.

Anne did attend school the next day, but she found it difficult to hide her grief.

Anne knew that Michael had made a will leaving her the house and contents. There was little money because Michael had had to make a financial settlement to his wife at the time of his divorce. The properties were like for like, but Michael's wife had taken early retirement whilst he was still working.

CHAPTER 58

A nne had telephoned Robert for him to come on the
Saturday that Michael collapsed, but Robert continued
to stay at the Isleworth house. It was not by invitation, but
of course it was more convenient for him to drive to ICL at
Putney! They still returned to Godalming at the weekend to
look after Beaumont House.

Anne noticed that Robert was suddenly becoming
extremely bad tempered. At Godalming he threw a cup
across the kitchen. Normally he played his cards very close
to his chest and hid his feelings well. He had in fact always
been *too* secretive.

Driving back to Isleworth from Beaumont House, Anne
could tell that something was seriously concerning him.

"What is wrong?" she asked. "Is there a problem with
your health?"

"No," replied Robert shortly.

"Well, is it your job?" she queried.

"Yes, I've been made redundant. I have to hand in the
Passat car and have to leave now in two weeks. I have to
transfer my redundancy payment into a pension so I shall
have no immediate income. The pension will not be available
until the time of my state pension."

Robert was now 53 so Anne could understand the
problem.

"Can you not get another position?" she enquired.

"There is a type of college called Chusid which is able to train people to find positions. It costs £500 but I can afford that. It offers a course, and teaches you all the skills needed to find employment."

"Well that seems the best thing to do. But you will have no car."

"I can use the car you traded in with Michael."

Michael had actually twice purchased Anne's car. Michael had bought her TR7 at trade price when she purchased her first Fiat X19. Since then she had purchased a later model and again Michael had bought her existing car at trade price.

Anne could see that Robert would need a car to travel to this college and possibly to search for further employment.

"When you leave ICL and hand in your Passat, I suppose it is sensible for you to drive Michael's car. It will only stand idle on the drive," she stated.

Anne then had another idea. "Your mother's house is standing empty. I suggest that you put it in good order when you leave ICL and rent it out. That will give you a monthly income at least."

Robert appeared relieved with these ideas and now accepted his situation with more equanimity.

Robert left his job. He joined the Recruitment Course for £500 and drove Michael's car. He employed a Letting Agency, who found tenants for his mother's house for £500 a month. He also managed to find some work with Census Forms. The Recruitment College seemed to propose using the 'Old Boys Network' which Robert deployed. He got in touch with an old colleague who was in charge of a Computer Consultancy Firm. He employed Robert at £2000 per month.

Robert was staying at the Isleworth house but made no contribution to the utilities. Neither was he paying anything at the Godalming House. He did occasionally buy some food.

Anne continued with the Masters Degree and once again was very occupied with study and research. Her days were spent with school, studying and maintaining the Isleworth and Godalming House.

Sadly, her father had a stroke. He became very frail and died from heart failure and pneumonia. Anne's mother could not cope with this, so Anne again had to arrange a funeral and then advertised for carers to look after her mother privately in her own home. Anne's mother had of course long since given up her shoe shop.

Anne now had to travel frequently to Wellingborough to organise payment for her mother's carers and to organise the garden and to buy her mother clothes, and items for the house that were needed. She visited Wellingborough every three weeks.

This pattern continued for some years. Robert was receiving income from rent and from his old colleague Brian who was running the Computer Consultancy Firm in London.

Anne obtained her Masters Degree but could proceed no further. Schools were now in charge of their own budgets and Anne could no longer spare the time for study. Many Headteachers in Hounslow retired at this time, but Anne soldiered on. It did mean that after the school day she had to check invoices and process cheques for payment. She seldom left school before 8pm.

It was time for another Ofsted Inspection. The present Deputy Head decided to leave, in lieu of this extra strain, and a new Deputy was appointed. He was also an excellent teacher and very supportive.

This Ofsted went well but not with quite such an accolade as previously. The Governing Body appeared to accept that the school would always have a good commendation. The Inspectors, however, were still congratulatory.

CHAPTER 59

The time came at last for Anne herself to retire. The head of an existing school in the Borough was appointed as the future Headteacher.

At Anne's farewell, over 100 parents, ex-pupils, who were in their 20s, and colleagues attended. This party was to be her nemesis.

A colleague from a local Comprehensive School came with two other members of the staff. They had all met when her children were invited to the Senior School to take part in some activities as a precursor to them actually attending the school in the September. Also to acclimatise them to secondary school life.

It was a good evening and the Director of Education made a speech thanking Anne for her dedication to the school. He listed some of the achievements accomplished by pupils during her time at the school. Over the years children had won a Police Panda Competition, won a first prize for Bhangra dancing, won first prize for an Environmental Exhibition, been in the finals for a Marks and Spencer Song Competition and of course obtained excellent Ofsted reports.

The staff had supplied all the catering. Anne was presented with a silver cake basket, a cut glass bowl and an amethyst pendant.

At the end of the evening, Anne invited the colleagues from the Secondary School to her home. They all had coffee and it was time to depart.

One of the male teachers, who had brought a female colleague, was concerned about time. It would be very late if he took her home. Anne immediately asked Robert if he would drive the lady teacher to her home in Chiswick. He agreed at once. Little did Anne know the ensuing consequences of this action.

During Anne's last year at the school, she had employed an Estate Agent to sell the Isleworth house. She loved the Isle of Wight, and had sailed round it on many previous occasions. Robert had long since sold his Heron sailing dinghy, but had purchased a share in a friend's boat and later completely purchased this. The boat was moored in Yarmouth harbour on the Isle of Wight. Some new houses were being built on the Island. Detached houses in the Tudor style. They were on the outskirts of Cowes. They visited the island and Anne resolved to purchase one of the houses. Anne put a deposit on the house she chose. It was near to completion and would be available within weeks.

When Anne finally left the school, the Isleworth house was sold, and the Isle of Wight house, as she hoped, was completed. The sale of the Isleworth house plus the lump sum from her retirement pension entirely covered the purchase price. It was a large house with spacious rooms, three bathrooms and with an excellent amount of ground.

Anne kept her Godalming house because from there it was an easier journey for visiting her mother. Sadly her father had died from a heart attack, and Anne had arranged the funeral.

Robert was of course still at work with the Management Computer Firm, so Anne stayed on the Isle of Wight to sort out the furniture when it arrived or the removal vans. They developed a pattern of staying at both houses. Anne had the garden at the new house designed with topiary, lawns and ponds, and enjoyed the time spent there.

She still travelled every three weeks to her mother from Godalming. She had purchased, on retirement, a little King Charles spaniel, also called Beaumont, and he travelled with her.

Robert was still making no financial contribution to either house but had now sold his own. He purchased a white SLK Mercedes car with some of the money from the sale of his mother's house and presumably invested the remainder of the money from his house sale. To Anne's amazement he suddenly seemed to be short of ready money.

"Are you still getting the £2000 a month from Brian?" Anne asked.

"Of course," he replied.

At Godalming he was still coming in at 8pm and sometimes on Friday evenings met her after he left work at Woking Station to travel to the Isle of Wight.

One Friday night after such a journey, she saw him talking on his mobile phone standing on the front terrace of the new house.

"To whom are you talking at this time of night?" she enquired.

"Oh a Tracy Edwards, I met her at a conference I recently went to."

Anne thought this very odd but dismissed the matter. The next day Robert informed her that he had to go to a Computer Conference in France for three days, the following week.

Anne queried this. "Why would a Conference last for three days?"

"It is three days and I can show you the paperwork," Robert said sharply. "It seems as if you do not believe I have to go."

They travelled back to Godalming and he did indeed leave for his trip to France for the three days. On his return he said little about the trip. Robert then began to say that he could not travel to the Isle of Wight on Friday evenings as before because he had meetings with clients in London. He always offered to show schedules and agendas. They began to travel to the Isle of Wight on Saturday instead.

It was Friday. Robert had again said he had a late meeting. Anne had not seen Robert unpack his case from his visit to France. He had left it in the garage. She was unpacking the case when she saw some envelopes in the side pocket. The envelopes were marked 'Robert!' Inside one envelope was a note.

Happy Anniversary Darling. Thank you for the most wonderful year of my life. All my Love. Gloria xxxx

Anne opened another envelope. Inside this was a postcard, the front of which was covered with printed condoms. On the back of the postcard was a message.

For condoms, substitute little blue pills. Love Gloria xxx

There was yet another envelope. This contained entry tickets to the Louvre and receipts that were obviously for French restaurants.

Anne was completely horrified. Anniversary! A year! An affair had clearly been taking place, once again without her knowledge. It was a complete body blow.

Anne could not believe this obviously passionate affair of which she was totally unaware had been taking place. There was the occasion that she had seen Robert with his mobile phone talking to a person, supposedly called Tracy Edwards, but he had passed this off as a trivial incident of no importance.

Anne was devastated. Gloria had apparently also travelled with Robert to France. Anne had, however, been rather suspicious of the strange Friday meetings. Most firms in London seemed only too happy to close early and many commuters had trains to catch, hoping to be home quickly for the weekend.

She thought about the postcard. 'Little blue pills' obviously meant Viagra. Anne had only seen advertisements for these and had read about concerns with side effects in the press.

For a year, Robert must have been involved in a full sexual relationship. In her wildest dreams Anne could not have imagined how, in time, it could all have taken place (apart of course from the French trip).

Anne thought Robert went to work at 8am. He always returned at 8pm and ate his meal. Anne had noticed, however, that he had been putting on weight, but thought he was having extra food when at work. Maybe nibbling biscuits, or having a Big Mac.

She was puzzled about the phrase 'The best year of my life'. The odd Friday evening and one trip to France hardly constituted 'the best year' of anyone's life. He was also always at the Isle of White house during the weekend, albeit they often travelled on Saturday.

She did, of course, visit her mother every three weeks, but it was only for a couple of days. Robert used to ring when she was there and always now met her upon her return either in London or Guildford. He then drove her home. Two days every three weeks seemed very little time for a passionate affair.

She just couldn't understand the words 'the best year of my life'. There seemed to be a piece of the jigsaw missing. Anne decided to phone Robert at the office.

"You seem to be having an affair with someone called Gloria. You left some incriminating envelopes in the case I was unpacking. I just cannot believe you are doing this to me again. I thought we had tried to put the past behind us."

Robert was silent. "What are you going to do?" he asked.

Anne noticed that he did not deny the affair.

"It's Friday," she said. "What are you going to do? Lately we seem to be going to the Island on Saturday, so I was expecting you home later tonight. I am going to the Isle of Wight now." Anne put down the phone. She just kept saying to herself, 'Not again'.

She tidied the house, locked up and, taking her dog, caught the bus to Guildford. She had to catch a train to Woking, and then a direct train to Southampton. She then caught a free bus to the Red Jet boat station, which took 25 minutes on the Solent to reach Cowes.

CHAPTER 60

A t Cowes she met a friend with whom Robert had sailed and from whom Robert had purchased the boat they had once shared. Sam could see that Anne was very upset. He was very kind and suggested she go with him to his home. He and his wife listened to her tale of woe and tried to comfort her. They had two little dogs, so Beaumont was cared for and happy, but Anne began to sob. It was just all too much. Over and over again Robert had let her down. Once she started to cry, she couldn't stop. She could see no way out of this situation. Gloria seemed firmly entrenched in Robert's life.

Sam and his wife did their best to calm her. She thanked them profusely for their kindness. Sam offered to drive her to Cowes. His home was in Totland on the far side of the island. As they drove to the house Anne saw that Robert was getting out of a taxi. Sam tactfully left.

They went into the house together and Anne fed her dog. Robert had brought some fresh milk and made some tea. Anne just didn't know what to say to him. Robert was obviously expecting to be asked to leave, although he had travelled there. He said that Gloria had told him that she would leave her phone on, and he could return to her at any time.

Anne thought long and hard. Did she want to be on her own? Jeremy was of course married and sadly Michael was dead. She had bought the Cowes house thinking that they would at last be contented. It was a lovely house on a lovely island. She had put considerable effort into making it a home to enjoy, but Robert always wanted more.

"How did it start?" she asked.

"If you remember, I gave Gloria a lift home after your retirement party. She gave me her phone number. When you visited your mother, I phoned her. We met for a drink and then I went to her flat and stayed the night. I suppose I am infatuated. We have formed a strong attachment."

Anne needed help. She phoned her cousin and told her about Robert's affair. Her cousin warned her, that although Anne owned both houses, if she divorced Robert, as they were married, a judge could still ensure that he received half of her assets. Her cousin also said, "There are many single women. Do you want to be one of them?" Her cousin was kind, however, and said that she could phone anytime. Anne could not think clearly.

Robert appeared very detached and said no more. He just found something to eat. Anne was not hungry. She just retired to bed.

The next morning Robert offered to take Beaumont for a walk. Anne guessed that he was going to phone Gloria.

They usually spent the weekends on the island working in the garden, sitting on the terrace or going to a nearby hotel for a meal. There were some nice beaches on which to walk, or on which Beaumont could play. On this occasion the time seemed to pass in slow motion.

Robert didn't say he wished to leave, and Anne did not pursue the matter, but Robert was definitely totally distracted. They survived the weekend and returned to Godalming. Still little was said.

As usual Robert left for work. Anne did phone two solicitors, who confirmed that Robert could indeed be awarded half of all her assets. Robert had signed two documents many years ago, stating that the Godalming house was hers and hers alone, but she was advised that this may be no longer valid.

She decided to phone Brian to see if Robert was indeed going to work. He seemed to be short of available cash these days. Robert was not at work. Brian said that there was insufficient work for Robert to now receive a salary. He had not paid Robert since the preceding December. He said that he asked Robert to continue working at the office and for them both to try hard to obtain other contracts. He said that Robert had made little effort. He was only coming into the office either for just the morning or sometimes not until later afternoon.

Anne told Brian how she had discovered his affair with Gloria. Brian confessed that he knew of the situation and Gloria had in fact phoned the office directly on at least six occasions. He said that Robert was always on his mobile phone when he was at the office. Brian stated that he had had several conversations with Robert condemning his behaviour and encouraging him to put effort into obtaining other prospects for their computer service. Brian promised Anne that he would inform her how things progressed at the office.

When Robert returned home at the usual time of 8pm, Anne informed him that she had spoken to Brian. He was not at all pleased by this information.

"When you are not at work, I presume that you are with Gloria," she stated.

"Not quite," he replied. "She had retired from school and undertakes private coaching in elocution. I just stay in the flat. We do go out for meals."

"Why don't you move in with her?" Anne decided to ask.

"She has many friends, and is very popular. I am afraid that she may tire of me. I don't really trust her to provide a permanent future. I know that she has had a previous marriage and several long-standing affairs."

The next day Robert left the house as usual at 8am. He had forgotten his mobile phone in his haste to leave. It buzzed. Anne switched it on. It was of course Gloria.

She heard this message:

"I can't wait for you to get here. I have a salad ready and waiting. I am longing to put my hands all over your body. Oh! Oh! Oh! Get here quickly, darling."

Anne felt nauseous. What a message. She found it hard to imagine anyone wanting to put their hands all over Robert's body. She had recently seen him coming naked out of the bathroom. He now had quite a protruding stomach.

Robert had removed some papers from his briefcase and placed them in a corner at the far end of the kitchen. Again with all the distressing scenes, he had forgotten to relocate and hide them. Anne looked through these. There were various Barclays Credit Statements. There were debts for several thousand pounds. Payments to a Thomas Winston, Marks and Spencer, Cruise Control, to name but a few. He had left his Bank Statements for the previous year. From October onwards he had started to withdraw £1000 a month and there were many payments to restaurants. One day alone there were two payments of £100 to a restaurant in Putney and one in Twickenham. 'Spinners', 'The Phoenix', 'The Taj Mahal', 'The Little Fox'. Seemingly on every day. Anne always provided an evening meal. It appeared that he was eating three large meals a day, which accounted for his obesity. He had even forgotten his cheque book which was in the pile of papers. For the preceding year there were payments to various Credit Companies. Many £500 payments to Barclays Credit Company, £500 to Access on different dates and £500 to American Express. The total amount for only three months was several thousand pounds. Anne puzzled how so much money could be spent.

When Anne asked how so much money could be spent in so short a time (the amounts she had seen were for the period of a few months), Robert replied that he could only recollect purchasing some emerald earrings and a handbag.

Anne was concerned at the large amount of money being spent on dining out. Robert was clearly gaining weight. He had only weighed 9st 13lbs when they were married, but now his weight was over 14 stone. He did admit that Gloria enjoyed visiting restaurants and he did not like to gainsay her. He was beginning to limp badly and Anne expressed concern at this. At first he was in denial, stating that he probably had corns on his toes, but finally realising that there was a problem he visited the doctor. The doctor discovered that ulcers had developed quite seriously on one foot. He was given an appointment to visit a podiatrist at the Royal Surrey Hospital. This treatment was for consecutive weeks. He did admit to meeting Gloria after these visits and again enjoying meals at various Surrey Hotels.

CHAPTER 61

Robert's walking became more difficult. Anne was so concerned that she suggested they consult a private specialist, which they did. Robert underwent CAT and MRI scans. They revealed arterial blockage in both legs due to Atherosclerosis. This was also found in his Aorta. An operation was suggested nicknamed a 'trouser operation', but this was a hazardous operation and Robert was very hesitant to commit to such a procedure.

Anne felt that these continued visits to restaurants was not helping the situation. She was also not sure if the continued taking of Viagra was having a negative effect on his health. She begged him to cease his relationship with Gloria. She felt that Gloria likened to Svengali from the George du Maurier novel Trilby (1895) who had a maleficent control over another. She suggested that Robert obtain psychiatric help. To her surprise he agreed, and this was arranged through his doctor. Appointments were made for him to be seen by a psychiatric nurse at Farnham Hospital in Surrey. Robert kept these appointments and brought home an interim report detailing his need to cease a disadvantageous relationship and his continuous need to be in contact with a certain lady. Anne felt that this was a fair assessment of the situation.

She had seen the O2 payments from his bank for his mobile phone. A continuous withdrawal of money to 'top up' his phone which indicated the inordinate amount of time he was in contact. She herself when walking Beaumont, had passed him talking on his phone, sitting in Michael's parked car. He had been totally unaware of her presence. She knew that he was totally infatuated with Gloria, but glad that he was obtaining help for this addiction.

The course of treatment ended, and a final report given that Robert could see the folly of continuing with this relationship. It was concluded that such a relationship was detrimental both to his mental well-being and to his physical health. Robert had admitted that there was difficulty in visiting his office to attempt work with Brian, travelling to visit Gloria and then travelling to Godalming and the Isle of Wight.

Anne hoped that there could be some closure now. She was aware that Robert seemed very happy and animated by this report. She had a flash of instinct.

"Have you been meeting Gloria after these visits to the hospital?" she enquired.

"Absolutely not. Don't be ridiculous. That would negate the whole purpose of the visits," Robert snapped.

Anne followed her instincts. She went to Robert's car. Inside was a copy of The Times newspaper. This was the paper favoured by Gloria.

"You have been meeting Gloria afterwards," she stated. "Look! You do not read The Times newspaper."

Robert just looked shamefaced and made no further denial.

"You only agreed to these meetings in order to further meet Gloria. You have wasted NHS money and resources," Anne stormed. "The whole involvement with the psychiatric team was, for you, just farcical."

Once again Robert had lied, not only to her, but to his doctor and the psychiatric team at Farnham. He clearly had no intention of ending this addictive relationship.

Anne was still, of course, visiting her mother every three weeks. She had to obtain Power of Attorney in order to obtain the money for her mother's care. Her dementia had increased and she now had four carers.

One weekend when at the Cowes house there was an urgent phone call from the main carer, Jane. She informed Anne that her mother had been violently sick and was now in Kettering Hospital. Anne left immediately with Beaumont. Anne hastily caught all the necessary transport to Wellingborough. Jane had returned from the hospital and felt that the situation was grave. Leaving Beaumont, Anne hired a taxi for Kettering Hospital. Jane was kind enough to accompany her.

It was clear her mother was seriously ill. She could not even retain the water that Anne persuaded her to drink. She was still alert, however, and said, "I don't want to die." Anne responded, "You are not going to. Medical help is not at its best during the weekends in hospital. The doctors will all come on Monday, and you will get better."

Anne really hoped that was the case, because she could see no doctor on the ward.

Jane and Anne returned to Wellingborough. Jane stayed with Anne but at 2.30am they received a phone call to return immediately to the hospital. Again, Anne called for a taxi but by the time they arrived, Anne's mother had died.

Once again Anne had to arrange a funeral. She contacted her mother's friends and relatives. Anne provided the money for the food, but Jane kindly organised all the catering for the wake at the house. Another carer, Sheila, volunteered to act as hostess. Anne knew that she was too traumatised to do this.

Anne had informed Robert and he drove to the house on the morning of the funeral, to be held in the afternoon. He was in the living room when his phone rang.

"Your phone is ringing," stated Anne.

"No, it is the radio from across the way. My phone is in my coat, which is now hanging in the hall cupboard."

He moved into the hallway. Anne guessed that he had two phones.

"Stop," she demanded. She patted his trouser pocket and removed the ringing phone. Of course, it was Gloria.

Anne was disgusted. Anne felt the lack of respect was dreadful. For Robert to allow it and for Gloria to do it, to ring on the day of her mother's funeral, was deplorable.

In the church, Anne would not walk behind the coffin with Robert, who was still limping badly. She walked with her cousin and held Jane's hand. She did not care where or what Robert was doing.

Robert did stay for the wake but then drove away. Anne remained at the house for a week. Her mother had already bequeathed the house to her. She would very much have liked to modernise it, and retain it, but this would involve remaining for a long period of time in Wellingborough. She could not trust Robert and Gloria and there were also the concerns about Robert's health.

She returned to Godalming, leaving Jane in charge of the house. Robert was still continually on his mobile phone.

Anne had of course consulted a solicitor in Wellingborough and probate was soon granted. Sadly, Anne put the Wellingborough house on the market. She could not, however, bear to also part with all the contents, so she decided to search for a small house on the Isle of Wight. She contacted several estate agents. One had just the house, a two bedroomed cottage with a lane leading to Totland Bay and to a wonderful view of the sea. The house in Lanes End.

She put a deposit on this house and purchased it immediately her mother's house was sold. Some very large items of furniture had to be taken to an Auction House, but she kept as many items as she could for the cottage. Jane disposed of her mother's clothes to charity and of course was given some of the less sentimental items from the house.

A removal firm was hired to take the remaining items to Lanes End. Anne decided to call the cottage Beaumont Cottage. She stayed at the cottage and Robert did come and stay with her. Beaumont the cavalier was also in residence.

Although Robert's walking was poor, he did in fact try to help, and soon Beaumont Cottage was looking a little bit like the Wellingborough House. Probably a miniature version of her mother's home.

CHAPTER 62

Robert's health was severely deteriorating. He could still drive, but was even having difficulty in walking to the train station for their visits to the Isle of Wight. It was obvious that something needed to be done. He again visited his own doctor who said that the problem was indeed atherosclerosis, causing a condition called claudication. This was prohibiting the blood flow to his legs. He urgently needed this 'trouser operation' mentioned by the private consultant. Failure to have this could mean the possible amputation of his legs. Robert was still partly in denial, but it was agreed that a date should be obtained for the operation to take place.

One day, Robert returned to the Godalming house looking very distressed. "I have informed Gloria of the impending operation and she is very displeased," he volunteered. "She is annoyed that I may not be able to visit for some weeks. She was not at all sympathetic or understanding. I am determined not to have contact with her again."

Anne found this hard to believe. Brian had told her that Robert was certainly spending more time at the office but often arrived there late or left early in order to spend time with Gloria. Brian had said that he still spent an inordinate amount of time on his mobile phone.

Now, however, Robert emphasised that enough was enough. The relationship was finally over. He said to Anne, "You will never know what it did to me, when she was so unconcerned about my welfare. I cannot forgive her."

When Anne asked several times if the relationship had really ended, he lifted one shoulder and repeated what he had said previously

The day came for the operation. They went to the hospital together. Robert had already had various tests including blood tests. They sat and waited. After three hours a bed was forthcoming. Robert was once again informed about all the possible serious consequences that could ensue from this operation and had to sign a document of consent. They were both extremely concerned. The operation was to take place the following day at 8am and would last for seven hours. The Registrar promised Anne that she would be phoned after the surgery.

Anne had to leave and wondered what news the next day would bring. She collected Beaumont from the gardener's wife, who had agreed, upon payment, to look after him when Anne was visiting at the hospital. Upon arrival at the gardener's house, Beaumont was brought out. Anne had secretly been hoping for a word of comfort or even the offer of a cup of tea, but none was forthcoming. She and Beaumont went back home and Anne had a heavy heart. She hadn't previously understood how very, very serious this operation appeared to be.

Several people telephoned her during the next day offering to come and stay with her. Two were friends who wished to bring their partners and one was her cousin. She declined the offers, as she knew that she would be visiting the hospital if all went well and did not wish for visitors.

At 5 o'clock, a nurse telephoned. She said that Robert was out of surgery and in the recovery unit. That seemed hopeful. Anne fed Beaumont, had a snack herself and went to bed. The hospital had a strict visiting schedule. Visitors were not allowed in until 2pm. After taking Beaumont to the gardener's wife, Anne drove to the hospital. Robert seemed very ill. She was informed that due to the operation, he may not be able to eat by mouth for at least three weeks. He seemed to have tubes coming out of him in all places and Anne was told that he was being taken into Intensive Care. Anne still stayed at the hospital that day until 8pm. She had to leave then and collect Beaumont.

She visited the hospital the next day but was shown into the Intensive Care Unit. She could not believe that it was Robert in the bed. There seemed to be even more tubes and of course a heart monitor. She was able to speak to him though.

"Should I phone Gloria?" she asked, thinking that she should be aware of this situation, knowing how close they had been.

"Don't do that," he managed to say. "It will only cause trouble."

Anne again stayed as long as she was allowed, but after collecting Beaumont, she felt that she should do the right thing and inform Gloria of the severity of the situation. She phoned the number from Robert's phone book. Gloria answered. Anne explained the situation. She was met with total derision.

"Of course I know all about it. Robert phoned me today from the Intensive Care Unit and told me that he loved me. The trouble is I shan't be able to see him for at least six weeks. Three weeks in hospital and three weeks convalescence. It's all such a nuisance. I shall ring him on the hospital bedside phone when it's available. Goodbye."

Anne was again stunned. She really had wanted to believe that he had ended this relationship, but it was obvious that yet again it was a lie. She was, however, still too concerned about him to worry about anything other than the success of the surgery.

The next day he was still ill, but out of Intensive Care. Again, she stayed until 8 o'clock. She made no comment about Gloria. He stated that he was concerned about a food tube that had been inserted into his neck. It had been reinserted by a new doctor and he didn't feel that all was well. He told her that he was frightened.

The following day when Anne visited, Robert was very ill indeed. He was hallucinating and fitting. Whilst she was there, at least eight nurses and doctors were treating him.

"Is he going to die?" Anne asked one Sister. There was no answer. He was apparently going back to the Intensive Care Unit. Anne couldn't cope. She told the sister, "If he dies, please don't inform me until the morning." She knew that if there was a further crisis, she was too drained to deal with it.

She returned home after collecting Beaumont. There was a sarcastic message on the phone from Gloria, but she deleted it as beneath contempt. Several of Robert's colleagues telephoned but none suggested they visit the hospital.

The next day she went straight to the Intensive Care Unit with trepidation. The male nurse in charge was smiling. "We have discovered the cause of what was a severe infection. It was caused by the food tube in his neck. It has been rectified and he can return to the ward."

Anne was delighted. Robert was euphoric, and as he was wheeled back to the normal ward he was waving at everyone he saw. He stayed in hospital for three weeks and Anne visited him every day. His only other visitor was the gardener.

CHAPTER 63

Robert was finally allowed home. Anne collected him from the hospital. He said that he desperately wanted Fish and Chips to eat, so Anne collected these from a nearby Fish and Chip shop.

He had to remain in bed for nearly three weeks, but he gradually regained his strength. He asked to sit in the garden room that had been built onto the house. (The money for this had been provided by Anne's parents.) Anne was happy for this to happen. It was at the rear of the house and he could see the garden. He seemed very happy to sit in this room, away from the main house. However, after he had retired to bed, she went in to rearrange the cushions. He had made a mistake, and on the table were two mobile phones that he must have been using.

Anne did feel some self-pity. She had visited him in hospital for often six hours a day. She had looked after him at home for nearly three weeks and obviously all he still wanted was to talk to Gloria. In fact, as soon as the doctor pronounced him fit, he drove off in the Fiat car. She knew where he was going to, of course – to Gloria.

Anne did not know to whom to turn. Even her cousin who had initially been so supportive was growing bored with the ongoing saga. She had no one to whom to turn as she had no children, no brothers or sisters, and both her parents dead. She nearly felt like phoning the Samaritans. Anthony, Jeremy's son, had very occasionally kept in contact and she had Jeremy's phone number. Was he still alive, she wondered. In desperation for some help she telephoned.

At first she did not recognise his voice. "Is Jeremy St Clare still alive," she asked tremulously.

"Very much so," the voice replied. "Could that be Anne? This is a blast from the past."

"Please don't put the phone down," begged Anne. "Are you able to talk?"

"My wife is at the hairdressers. What is wrong?"

Anne tried to tell him as briefly as possible about Robert's latest affair with Gloria and his recent brush with death. Jeremy had once said that he would always be her anchor and he did not let her down. He promised that he would telephone her when possible and tried to comfort her. Anne knew that it was very wrong of her to ring, but she had almost been at breaking point with all that had occurred.

She did tell Robert that she had telephoned Jeremy who now apparently lived in Scotland. Robert must have informed Gloria of this, because a few days later there was a message on her answer phone.

"Robert has told me that you have a boyfriend in Scotland. It sounds like a Mills and Boon story. I have never heard such rubbish. Ha! Ha! Ha! Who could possibly want you?"

Anne just deleted the message. Brian was closing down his Computer Management Company. There had been no assistance in obtaining new contracts from Robert, even when he was well, and it was no longer a viable concern. Boxes of documents and some of Robert's possessions were being relocated to his house in Byfleet. He suggested that Robert visit, collect any possessions, but maybe they could still attempt to activate some work from his home.

Robert had realised the firm was failing. Although Robert had received no salary (this was a lesser burden to the company), Brian had clearly been struggling to obtain any lucrative work. They had a chat on the mainline phone at Godalming and Robert agreed to visit Brian in his home. He initially collected some personal items and then continued to visit. Brian contacted Anne.

"I am sorry, Anne, but the visits from Robert must stop. He is doing little here, and I have heard him on his mobile phone talking to Gloria. He is just coming here briefly then meeting her at Ripley, I believe for a meal. I am sorry to inform you of this. Robert has such a good brain, but he really is behaving in such a foolish way. I liken Gloria to a condor who has Robert as prey in its sights. She seems relentless and he totally besotted."

Anne thanked him and wished him well. Robert could no longer visit Brian, so his means of escape were now limited.

Anne was so tired of the whole debacle that she did ask Robert to leave. Some time ago she had persuaded Robert to visit a solicitor on the Isle of Wight and again sign a document disclaiming any rights to her assets. This had been witnessed. She was still unsure if a post-nuptial agreement had the validity of a pre-nuptial agreement, but she really felt that the continuance of this frenetic affair was having a detrimental effect on her mental health. Robert said that he was not leaving.

"But in effect you leave every day," Anne protested. "Sometimes you are ringing every two hours. The phone is continually buzzing here. You have no interest in me or the houses. Since your operation you do no gardening. I have to obtain outside help for maintenance within the homes. If you are not on your phone, you are writing messages on your iPad. You are not really here. Why won't you leave?"

Robert stubbornly insisted that he was not going anywhere.

Within days, Anne's landline phone rang when at their house on the Isle of Wight. Robert had driven Anne there. He had recovered well, but found the journey easier by car.

"Hello, it's Gloria. If you want Robert to leave, I want a property and a lump sum." (Anne noticed that she said "I".)

"What do you mean by a lump sum?" asked Anne.

"Oh – a hundred thousand."

Robert walked in. "Please discuss this with Robert," retorted Anne. She handed Robert the phone and walked away.

She had no idea what was said. She could only guess that Robert had told Gloria that she wanted him to leave. Gloria possibly felt that Robert was too cowardly to make any demands and to avoid huge solicitors' fees, thought it could be settled between themselves.

Anne felt that even if she did agree to this deal, there was no guarantee that once Gloria had been granted her request, she would remain faithful to Robert. Once she had the proceeds from the sale of a house and the £100,000, who knows what could happen. Robert would never contest her for any return.

Anne decided to dismiss the matter entirely. Gloria now knew that there were three houses as assets and clearly wished to manipulate Robert to gain access to some of these.

Robert dismissed the whole conversation with the words, "She was just flying a kite" – whatever that was supposed to mean. Anne decided it was pointless asking him to leave.

Her mother had purchased Kenilworth for her after Robert had left and this had become Cranleigh. She had initially struggled without financial help to maintain this property.

Only due to Michael's kindness had she been able to purchase the house at Cowes. Beaumont Cottage was purchased from the sale of her mother's house. All had involved hard work and effort. She was not prepared to relinquish anything.

CHAPTER 64

Jeremy, as promised, did ring Anne from time to time. He remembered only too well how he had felt when in the aftermath of Christine leaving. He listened to the continuing saga of Robert and Gloria, but he had some worries of his own.

When Anne was with him, he had smoked a pipe. His wife Charmaine smoked cigarettes. This concerned him and apparently he tried to make a pact that they both gave up smoking. Jeremy did this, but Charmaine could not break the habit. Recently she had been getting very out of breath. She had been tested with Spirometry, a simple test for lung function, and this had revealed Chronic Obstructive Pulmonary Disorder. This meant regular visits to a clinic. She had been presented with a bronchodilator and Roflunilast to decrease airway inflammation, but needed regular checks on her breathing capacity.

Jeremy was very concerned because she did not seem at all well. He sent Anne photographs of his cottage in Lockerbie. It rested in some hills that were covered in sheep. The cottage itself looked enchanting, and to Anne's surprise, the garden was lovely. It had waterfalls and ponds, sculptures and statues, and a well-designed summer house. It was all very picturesque. Anne was happy that he had found his dream home.

Now that Robert had recovered from his operation and his mobility was again back to normal, they now always travelled to the Island by train and of course boat. Suddenly, waiting for the Red Jet on a return journey to Godalming, Robert complained of chest pains. These seemed to ease but then started again. Anne gave Robert some Aspirin, which helped him, until they reached home. The pains started again but faded after Robert drank some sweet tea.

The next morning Robert informed Anne that he thought he should visit the doctor. He obtained an urgent appointment. Following an electrocardiogram, the GP was sufficiently concerned to refer Robert to a cardiologist at the Royal Surrey hospital. The appointment quickly came through. Robert went on his own and Anne stayed with Beaumont at the house.

When Robert returned, he informed her that he had been tested with an echocardiogram and undergone angiography. He added that the cardiologist, Mr Streatham, had discovered narrowed arteries in his heart. Mr Streatham was arranging for Robert to have at least one stent fitted at the Royal Brompton Hospital in Chelsea. This coronary angioplasty could last for between 30 minutes to two hours, but would involve an overnight stay.

Again, the appointment came through quickly. Robert drove to Guildford Station and took the train to London. He told Anne not to visit, as it was only an overnight stay and Gloria was going to visit in the evening.

Robert returned. He actually had two stents fitted and was grateful to Mr Streatham and the care he had received. He was also happy because he said Gloria had visited as promised in the evening following the procedure. He said that she was on her way to the Opera.

Unfortunately, once again, upon return from the Island, Robert again had Angina. This time Robert was able to contact Mr Streatham directly, who was sufficiently concerned to make an immediate appointment at the Royal Brompton

Hospital. Again, Robert left on his own in the early morning. He joyfully told Anne that Gloria had promised to visit once again.

At 9.30pm the telephone rang at the Godalming House. Anne answered. It was Robert. In a forlorn voice he said, "She didn't come. She rang to say she had an urgent appointment."

Anne was not concerned about this. "What type of treatment did you have?" she enquired.

"Oh I had another stent. I have three now. They found another narrowed artery."

"How do you feel?"

"Oh I'm fine. I just can't understand why Gloria didn't come as promised."

"Silly man," thought Anne, as she said Goodnight and hung up the phone. "He's more concerned about Gloria than his own health." Robert's obsession with Gloria was never ending.

The next day Robert returned, but she had a telephone call from Anthony, Jeremy's younger son.

"Dad's had a stroke," he said. "Charmaine has phoned to say that he is in hospital in Glasgow." He told her the hospital and even the name of the ward, Kistrel.

"I am so sorry," said Anne. "When did it occur?"

"Charmaine was giving Dad a cup of tea and it just slipped through his fingers. He lost strength in his arm. Charmaine rang 999. I am going up to see him and will keep you informed."

"Thank you so much," replied Anne.

The next day Anthony phoned from his mobile. He was in Scotland. "It was a problem with the carotid artery," he reported. "It's ok. They seem to have fixed the problem and it's under control. He'll only be in for a couple of days. I am very upset, however, Charmaine will not let me stay at the house. She says she is worried and cannot cope. I'm driving home as it seems Dad will be ok."

Anne could tell that Anthony was very upset. She wished him a safe journey. The next day she rang the hospital and asked to speak to Mr St Clare.

"Who's calling?" they asked.

Anne did not want to give her name in case it was reported to Charmaine.

"Mrs Anchor," she said.

The nurse obviously had to ask Jeremy if he wished to speak to 'Mrs Anchor'. He knew at once who it was and agreed. The nurse gave him the mobile phone. His speech was slightly slurred, but his brain was working well. "I'm fine," he said. "Soon be home. She wouldn't let Anthony stay at the house. Can't forgive that. He's my son. Came all the way up here."

Anne was grateful that he could speak and was on the way to recovery. He was so lucky that the problem was diagnosed so quickly. She of course wished him well.

"Everyone seems to have health problems," she thought prosaically. Robert with Angina, Charmaine with COPD and now poor Jeremy with a problem from his carotid artery.

As she mused, she could see Robert crouched in the car and of course, talking on his mobile phone.

Anne herself began to find difficulty in walking. She had sensed a problem for some time. Her right knee and hip felt strained and she had dismissed this. She had always felt this strain when pushing her mother in the wheelchair. She too, however, visited the doctor and she was referred to the Royal Surrey. After X-ray and blood tests, she was informed that she required a hip replacement. As her mother had once undergone similar surgery with little problem, Anne was unconcerned. Luckily, although she was not a private patient, an appointment came through quickly.

Robert drove her to the hospital on a Wednesday. He said he could not stay because of the dog. Anne did begin to feel some trepidation. A nurse marked her hip with a big black cross. The operation was to be the next day. She asked a nurse to stay with her on the way to the theatre as she began to feel frightened. Someone with a green head covering came to hold her hand and she knew no more.

When coming round in the Recovery Room, Anne could hear herself babbling about Gloria. Although she was lightheaded, she could hear the words pouring out. She was taken to a ward and put onto a morphine drip. She became more conscious. It was Thursday and now visiting time. Robert did not come but sent a message via a nurse wishing her well. Anne began to shake. Her drip came out and spilled over the bed. She was weak and her body was still in shock from the operation, but she still realised that Robert was with Gloria, probably taking her for yet another meal. Most husbands would be with their wives, at this time, but yet once again he was conspicuously absent.

He appeared almost before the end of visiting time and only stayed for 20 minutes. Her sheets had been changed and she had been tended to, but still on the morphine drip. Robert said little, but said he couldn't stay because the dog was in the car.

By Friday Anne was able to leave the bed. The drips all disconnected. She was able to walk unaided to the toilet. At the 2 o'clock visiting time, visitors poured into the ward, but no Robert. He came for a short time at 6.30pm. His excuse was always that he couldn't leave Beaumont.

Saturday, again no Robert at 2pm and the same on Sunday. On Sunday she was able to walk down a corridor. She found a television room. The TV was on, but no one else was in the room. They were obviously with friends and family in the wards. Anne watched 'Mutiny on the Bounty' on her own, to pass the time. Robert appeared again at 6.30pm. He told her the doctors had informed him she could be collected at 2pm the next day.

On Monday she had a little physiotherapy i.e. walking up and down four wooden steps, was given a stick and dressed to be ready to be discharged. Robert did arrive and after a wait for some prescription drugs, drove her home. As she hobbled into the house, she heard the phone ringing, but it stopped. She just guessed it was Gloria trying to check if she was there.

The house was totally neglected. It looked untidy and the floor required vacuuming. She felt too poorly to do anything about this, but managed to telephone the gardener's wife and ask for help. The lady came. She helped Anne to bed and soon cleared the mess. She provided some food. Robert stayed at the house, but Anne could not tell what he was doing. She gathered the dog was fed though.

The gardener's wife came the next day as well. Robert left to do some shopping, but also probably to phone Gloria.

Anne was just able to manage the stairs, but her leg was extremely swollen and she moved with difficulty. She looked at the garden. That too needed care, so she asked the gardener's wife if her husband would organise this. Anne paid for all the work.

She managed to walk Beaumont using her stick and walking very slowly. The dog seemed to understand and kept pace with her.

Anne was deeply hurt. She had stayed with Robert when he was in hospital, for his arterial bypass, for 5-6 hours a day. She hadn't visited him in Brompton at his request. She had felt so neglected when friends and relatives came to visit in the ward. Robert had only stayed for 30 minutes.

Anne had had no friends to visit because the majority were either in London or Isleworth where she had spent many years, but Robert should have been there for her.

Jeremy did phone her at Godalming. He had long since been discharged from hospital, but as he was at home, Anne had not been able to contact him. It was some considerable time since he had contacted her. Indeed, due to circumstances and health problems, they had not been in contact for several months.

Anne informed Jeremy about her hip operation, but he had some bad news. He had been diagnosed with polycythemia, an overproduction of red blood cells. He was being taken by car, provided by the NHS, fairly regularly for treatment at the hospital in Glasgow. Anne was very sorry to hear this. She looked up 'polycythemia' in her medical book and the prognosis for life expectancy was 3-5 years. Anne was deeply saddened.

Robert drove Anne to the Isle of Wight, and she was able to walk now a little better.

Anne decided that she needed a holiday. She decided to book a cruise with P&O which conveniently had cruise ships leaving from Southampton Docks. Robert was pleased to do this, but of course it was she that paid. Beaumont was to go to kennels. The cruise was for eight days to Guernsey, France and Lisbon. They packed and Robert took Beaumont to the kennels.

They travelled on the Red Jet and then by taxi to the Mayflower Dock. The embarkation procedure was tortuous, but once on board, in their cabin, Anne was able to relax. She could not walk well, but on board were many lifts. The food was excellent, and Anne enjoyed the 'Black Tie' evenings, when she could wear the evening dresses she had packed. Robert did look well in his dinner suit. They booked to go on coach tours, but at Guernsey they were moored a long way out and had to wait for boats to take them ashore, and to return, which was very tedious.

The boat anchored in Lisbon and Cherbourg. The coach trips were well organised, providing a good tour of the cities and surrounding countryside. When the coach stopped for breaks, however, Robert was always using his mobile phone.

Anne gathered from Robert that Gloria's circle of friends had widened. He seemed desperately worried that he may no longer to be the number one.

When they returned home, Robert of course collected Beaumont. His desperation became more apparent. He spent hours on his laptop and iPad, leaving her as usual to look after the house and the garden. It was a large garden and even with a topiary gardener, and a gardener to do the mowing, there was still much to do.

Anne did see one message from Gloria with the words 'Keep loving me', but it did not say 'I love you'.

Robert admitted that he needed to send more presents to Gloria, in his words "to fight off all the others". He seemed almost demented and he made no attempt to hide his concern.

Another sad event occurred: Robert's Aunt Doris died. He felt that he must attend the funeral. She had moved to a care home in Norfolk near to her niece, but although not 100% fit, he said that he must attend. Anne understood this and put out his dark suit and black tie. His cousin told him the time and place of the funeral and he left at 10am to meet up with his cousin. Anne understood that the funeral was at 1.30pm. Robert arrived home at 9.30pm and Anne queried this.

Robert became nasty. "You have no idea of the journey," he snarled. "It is a very complex trip." Robert said nothing about the funeral, and made no comment about the wake.

Anne was suspicious and phoned Barbara, Howard's cousin. She expressed condolence but Barbara was upset.

"Robert left immediately after the cremation, and wouldn't stay for the wake at our house," she complained.

"Goodness," said Anne. "What time did he leave?"

"Before 2.30pm. He obviously wanted to get home."

Anne said nothing, but she knew what he had done. He had left to visit Gloria.

Anne tackled him about this and he confessed that he had taken a train from Norfolk to Surbiton and then a taxi to Gloria's. Gloria had driven him back to Surbiton when he caught a train to Guildford and drove home.

Anne had half guessed he would use this time to meet Gloria, but had thought they would meet at Waterloo for a drink maybe. She should have guessed he would manoeuvre a visit, because his behaviour was always so devious. He couldn't even spare time to mourn his Aunt Doris, whom his mother had loved.

Anne let the matter drop. It was yet another twist in Robert's deceptive life.

Another very sad thing occurred for Anne: Beaumont died. He had been slowing down, but had gone into the garden with Robert. He came into the house, sighed and died. Robert insisted that he wasn't dead, but Anne knew otherwise. Robert was being Robert the ostrich. They arranged for 'Pets at Rest' to take Beaumont away. Before he went, Anne brushed his coat and ears and said a tearful goodbye.

Anne needed a companion and wanted another dog. They tried Animal Rescue for a King Charles Cavalier, but there were none available. One helpful lady on the internet suggested a breeder in Colchester. They phoned the number and amazingly a Blenheim King Charles Cavalier of eight weeks was available. Anne offered to fetch the dog by train, but Robert offered to drive. It was a long drive there and back, but Robert had obtained the puppy for £750. Robert was very weary when he arrived with the puppy (it had been provided with a carry cage), and fell quite heavily on the drive. It made Anne realise that they were both getting older and not as fit as hitherto. Anne noticed that imperceptibly Robert was slowing down.

They returned to Godalming as usual, but the puppy, still named Beaumont, in honour of his predecessor, needed to be carried until he had received all his vaccinations.

The puppy's kennel name was Pascavale Banjo and his mother had apparently won best puppy in breed at Crufts. He had only been available because the lozenge on his head was not central. He was a very arrogant little dog, and appeared to know that he was a pedigree.

Poor old Robert was still frantically sending Gloria messages on his iPad, and presents. He admitted sending £50 for a silver bracelet that Gloria hinted she would like. He also mentioned that Gloria has mentioned equity release. Gloria owned her own flat and received the state pension and a teacher's pension. At first Robert discussed the idea with her and even made some telephone calls to ascertain what was involved, but even he felt that it was a ruse to extract money from him.

Chapter 65

Jeremy phoned with some dreadful news. His wife had terminal lung cancer and had been told that she would only have three months to live. He was furious with the doctor who told her this and made a strong complaint to their surgery. He said that the Hippocratic oath said 'Do no harm', and harm had been done to his wife. She was naturally obviously completely devastated. Macmillan nurses had been contacted.

Anne knew that the doctors were compelled to tell patients the prognosis, but Jeremy was beside himself with grief. His wife was now supplied with oxygen through tanks in the house. Jeremy's two sons were saddened for their father, but had not had a good relationship with their stepmother. Ironically, their own mother had died from a similar disease many years ago.

One night Jeremy phoned Anne and said, "I am on my own now." He meant this in sorrow. It was how he had felt many, many years ago after Christine left after his jealous temper. He had a funeral to arrange. Jeremy had never been a rich man, but Charmaine had put £10,000 from the sale of her house into a ring-fenced bank account for their funerals.

Jeremy chose a large hotel in Lockerbie for the wake, and said there were 30 cars in the funeral cortege. It was the custom in Scotland for the coffin to be in the church the preceding night. Jeremy said that he went to the church and kissed Charmaine goodbye. She had been a good wife to him, and she had loved him. Anne knew how deeply he grieved.

There was another blow, however, for Jeremy. His own family returned to his cottage after the wake, including Charmaine's only son, who dropped the bombshell that his mother had made a will leaving half of the house to him. Jeremy's sons were furious that this should be mentioned at this tragic time, as Jeremy wondered if her son was going to immediately claim his inheritance, leaving him practically homeless. There was apparently a very unpleasant atmosphere at the end of this very sad day.

After a period of time, Jeremy asked Anne if she would like to visit. Many years ago she and Jeremy had visited a friend who had such a cottage. At that time, he had said how he wished such a cottage was his. Anne very much wished to see what had been the fulfilment of his dream. She decided to go. She informed Robert that she would be away for three days and he agreed to look after the new Beaumont.

Anne couldn't resist saying, "I am sure you will see Gloria."

"Don't be ridiculous," he retorted.

Anne left from Southampton. She was very worried about the journey. She had to change at Birmingham and Carlisle and was worried about changing platforms and catching the connections. It was a long journey, six hours, but Jeremy was waiting at Lockerbie Station in his car. Anne had suggested that she paid for the meal as he was providing the board. They went to a hotel for a very appetising meal. Afterwards, Jeremy drove Anne from Lockerbie to his cottage. Anne was entranced with the scenery. Water, hills, sheep and no traffic on the journey. Jeremy's house was even better in reality than the photographs had portrayed. There was a long drive to the cottage, with a delightful garden wrapping itself around the house.

Inside was magnificent. Wooden beams, made by Jeremy, in the ceiling and the most wonderful hand carved furniture, polished to a bright sheen. There was an elaborately carved fireplace in the living and dining room. The kitchen was perfect with handmade doors by Jeremy. All the floors were covered with tiles that Jeremy had researched from a firm in the Lake District. Anne could happily have lived in this cottage herself. A nearby farmer came to call and the time soon passed. Anne did sleep with Jeremy, but they just cuddled up together.

The next day Jeremy was impatient to show Anne some local lochs and waterfalls. They ate out for lunch and tea. When they arrived back at the cottage, the farmer, his wife and a friend called in. Anne explained that they had been friends many years ago.

The day came for departure. Anne was sorry to leave. It had been lovely seeing Jeremy again, but how he had changed. Once he had looked rather like a film star, Cary Grant or Gregory Peck. Now his head was shaved and he had a beard and moustache. When she had last been with him, he had worn a blazer and smart trousers; now he wore a loud check shirt, a canvas jacket and baggy trousers. He had to wear big boots because his instep had collapsed after the childhood injury. He was still the man she had known, however, and they talked well into the night. Again they slept in the same bed.

Jeremy drove her to the station. His sister was coming to stay with him, so Anne felt comforted that he would have company.

The journey home seemed very long, but Robert did meet her from the boat at Cowes with Beaumont. They went for a drink. Anne told Robert about the delightful scenery and the wonderful furniture, hand carved and polished by Jeremy.

She asked him what he had done. He said he'd been to see the boat now moored in East Cowes and walked the puppy who had now had his vaccinations.

Anne noticed black streaks along the side of his car. "Why is your car so dirty?" she asked.

"It rained at the boat yard," he replied, "and dirt splashed up."

Anne was not convinced. She had become perceptive where Robert was concerned. "They look like the marks from someone driving on a motorway," she insisted.

"I haven't been anywhere," Robert insisted.

Anne could hardly complain if he had, as she had been to see Jeremy, but she preferred the truth. When his bank statement came, Anne hid it. She took it upstairs and read it. There was the amount of £76 for the Red Funnel, which was the cost to transport a car across the Solent. Anne confronted him. "Why can't you tell the truth? You did go to meet Gloria. I cannot complain because I went to see Jeremy, but why lie?"

"OK, I did go. I met Gloria at Ripley and we had a meal."

Anne did not know if this was true either. He could have driven to Gloria's flat.

"What about Beaumont?" she asked.

"Well, he came with me," Robert answered.

Anne didn't ask how the puppy was fed or how he travelled in the car. Robert was so skilled at inventing every answer to suit the occasion.

They returned to Godalming. Anne noticed an envelope in the bottom of a shopping bag. Robert had forgotten to post it as it was stamped. It was addressed to Gloria. She passed it to Robert who wryly returned it to her. She opened it.

"I am so glad you found the fine tables. The enclosed is to pay for them, dearest one.

All my love as ever

R xxxxxxxxx

The cheque was for £140.

Obviously Gloria had mentioned purchasing these at their meeting and perhaps Robert hadn't taken his cheque book with him.

Anne reminisced on all the lies Robert had told over the past years, and how every occasion had been spoiled by his devotion to Gloria.

They had belonged to the Island Sailing Club, and the evening functions there were marvellous, but upon returning home, Robert was always on his mobile phone texting messages of love and devotion to Gloria. She had found him typing these on many occasions. If they went for a meal locally, only for a snack, he would suggest that she walk home with the dog in order to drive via another route to ring Gloria. Anne felt that it had all been so ridiculous and this time, she really did urge him to leave.

"Ask Gloria if you can stay with her," she argued. "Why keep ringing and ringing when you could be there all the time. Ask her if you can go to her?"

Robert said that he would do this and went out in his car. He returned. Whether or not it was the truth Anne could never know, but he said that Gloria said that it may not work out if they were always together. She added, he said, that in any case her flat was too small for them both to live in. How could Anne know if this had really been Gloria's answers?

Roberts's finances were now depleted. Thousands of pounds had been given to Gloria in presents, or directly in cash. His credit statements had shown large sums of dollars transferred to her when she visited her sister in America. There were payments to holiday firms of which Anne had no knowledge. He could no longer afford to live on his own, as rents were high, and his pensions small. Anne had to forget the idea of him leaving, as he had nowhere to go.

Chapter 66

Jeremy's health was clearly failing, and Anne did visit him yet once more. His sister had been with him to help. A nurse was visiting twice a day for injections. He could still drive and as before they went for a meal at a local hotel in Lockerbie.

The following day, however, he was clearly unwell. Some friends visited and stayed for most of the day. Anne did say that she only had this one day with him, but they still stayed. Anne bought some food from a little travelling shop and catered for everybody. Jeremy was asleep in his chair as they left, and Anne ordered a taxi to take her to the station the following day. She did not see him again.

She did phone him when she returned home (whether or not Robert visited Gloria she did not know), and he was waiting for an ambulance to take him to hospital. The next day she managed to find the ward to which he was admitted and telephoned. The sister answered the phone. Anne realised that the situation was grave, but she was not a relative. She told the sister that once they had been lovers. She was informed that he had little time to live and permitted Anne to speak to him on her phone. Anne asked Jeremy if he would like to see his sons and he said, "That would be nice." She then said, "I love you."

He replied, "I know."

"I hope you have thought something of me," she said.

"A hell of a lot," he answered.

They were the last words she ever heard from him.

She telephoned Anthony and urged he and his brother to travel to the hospital as soon as possible. She informed Anthony that the Sister had explained that Jeremy had little time to live. They were at the hospital within hours and William spoke to her on the phone stating that his father had expressed a wish for a certain minister to preside at his funeral. Anthony informed Anne when his father died.

Anne did not go to Lockerbie for the funeral, but sent a heart shaped wreath of red roses with a simple message thanking him for the friendship they had once shared.

Eventually, Jeremy's cottage was sold. Charmaine's son had the half share willed to him, and William and Anthony a quarter share each.

Chapter 67

Anne began to notice that Robert was dragging his feet. Also he was driving her to Beaumont Cottage one day and appeared fixated. He would not move over on the road to allow another driver to pass. This driver shouted and swore at him. Anne decided that she would not be a passenger in his car again.

Shortly afterwards, when driving to collect some plants from a nursery, he returned with the side of the car smashed in. He had driven into some chicanery poles in the road. Fortunately he was uninjured. They knew a very good car mechanic and he rebuilt the damaged car fairly quickly. Anne helped to pay the bill for the repair.

This happened again. This time Robert hit the pole at a Pelican crossing. The car was almost a write-off, but the same mechanic, gifted with car repairs, said that he could repair it, but it would be very expensive. Anne checked with the Insurance Company and there was an excess of £1000. It was pointless making a claim as this was the car that Robert had purchased from the sale of his parents' house. It was 18 years old.

Anne purchased a little Mazda, in which he could go shopping, but she would not travel with him.

To travel to the Isle of Wight they began to hire a taxi to collect them from the house to Woking station, and similarly in reverse.

Robert became slow at eating, as well as slow in walking. Anne persuaded Robert to visit his doctor, who suggested he consult with a private specialist at the Nuffield Hospital in Surrey. His doctor suspected Parkinson's Disease, but was not totally convinced.

Anne and Robert went by taxi to the Nuffield Hospital. Robert underwent various tests and the consultant confirmed that Robert had indeed got Parkinson's disease. He was also put onto a heart monitor, and they were told that he also had Ischemic Heart Disease, and a faulty valve. The specialist was a kindly man, who unfortunately was near to retirement. Anne confided in him the lifestyle that Robert had lived. The triangle of rushing from work in Redhill, to see Gloria in Twickenham, and back to Godalming, consuming several meals in a day and frequently taking double strength Viagra, the specialist stated that this lifestyle had undoubtedly caused all Robert's health problems. He asked Robert if he was still in touch with Gloria. Robert did not answer, but Anne confirmed that indeed he was.

"Well, you will stop ringing, won't you?" said the elderly specialist, kindly attempting to help.

Robert made no reply. He was prescribed with Sinamet pills to slow the advance of Parkinson's and they left for home.

Despite his slowing mobility, Robert was determined to ring Gloria as often as possible. Using the excuse of dog walking, he set off out for the seafront. He was so engrossed in his conversation on the mobile that he omitted to see some concrete poles situated to deter cyclists, near to a small seafront kiosk. He fell onto the poles and hit the concrete surface of the promenade. This was witnessed by a neighbour who helped him to his feet, and caught the dog.

Robert told Anne of the accident, but said he was only slightly bruised. The neighbour phoned to inquire if Robert was alright, and Anne thanked her.

It was not until the next morning that Robert started to have difficulty breathing. Anne phoned 111 and asked for a paramedic. Unfortunately, due to a serious emergency no one arrived until 6pm. By this time Robert was gasping for breath. An ambulance was sent for and Anne was advised to stay behind with Beaumont. She was advised that an X-ray would be forthcoming.

Anne phoned the hospital but it was not until 2am that she was informed Robert was now in the X-ray unit, but to contact them in the morning.

Leaving Beaumont in the house, Anne went to the hospital by taxi. Robert was still in the Assessment Unit but Anne was told that he had seven broken ribs and one had partially damaged his lung. He was taken to a ward and put onto oxygen.

Anne phoned a friend to sit with Beaumont and visited the hospital every day for ten days. Robert came home, but this experience caused deterioration in his health. It took several weeks for his ribs to heal.

Ironically, he then fell out of bed, and again broke five ribs. This time again he went to hospital. Anne did phone Gloria, and asked her to ring Robert. Anne could not visit the hospital which now had many patients with Covid. Anne was also very concerned that Robert would catch Covid.

Anne thought that speaking to Gloria may improve his spirits and hasten his recovery. Gloria was reasonably civil, probably for the first time, but Anne knew from Facebook and Twitter, that Gloria had a very wide circle of friends and despite Robert's obsession with her, she was not obsessed with him.

Robert came home immediately his need for oxygen ceased, due to the pandemic, but the broken ribs caused a further decline in his health.

He was of course delighted that Gloria had phoned him in hospital. He had his mobile phone with him and was still ever hopeful that in Gloria's world, he was number one.

Robert was banned from driving, as his health deteriorated further. He dribbled with his food and his clothes required daily washing. He lost weight and was now bent over in the Simeon stoop, particular to the disease. He required Sinamet four times a day. This is a mix of levodopa and carbidopa. These help to combat the loss of dopamine in the brain.

Anne looked at this poor, thin, bent figure that was now Robert. She had once seen him hurdling at university. He had bragged to her when driving to and from Gloria's flat in Twickenham to Godalming, 'Driving is nothing to me', but now he had great difficulty in even walking. She remembered the story of Dorian Gray, a philosophical novel depicting the change in the portrait of Dorian Gray as he lived a dissipated and degenerate lifestyle. The resulting painting was a hideous caricature of a once handsome man. She could liken Robert to this unfortunate portrayal.

Despite all that had happened, Robert's hair needed cutting. Barbers were closed due to the Pandemic, so Anne came to the rescue. Anne trimmed Robert's hair and his beard. He was unable to trim this himself. He looked smart, but was still in his pyjamas. Dressing was now difficult.

Classic FM played 'Invitation to the Dance' by Carl Weber (1819). In this, the story 'of two dancers who bow and curtsey in the finale and go their separate ways'.

Anne took Robert's hand, and held him in waltz position. Whilst he could only do a few steps Anne danced around him. They had not completely gone their separate ways and were still together.

'Love is not love
Which alters when it alteration finds
Or bends with the remover to remove
O no! it is an ever fixed mark
That looks on tempests and is never shaken.'

William Shakespeare Sonnet 116

www.ingramcontent.com/pod-product-compliance
Lightning Source LLC
Chambersburg PA
CBHW032031040426
42449CB00007B/856